T0214724

The Definitive Guide to PCI DSS Version 4

Documentation, Compliance, and Management

Arthur B. Cooper Jr.
Jeff Hall
David Mundhenk
Ben Rothke

Foreword by Bob Russo, Former General Manager,
PCI Security Standards Council

Apress®

The Definitive Guide to PCI DSS Version 4: Documentation, Compliance, and Management

Arthur B. Cooper Jr.
Colorado Springs, CO, USA

David Mundhenk
Austin, TX, USA

Jeff Hall
Minneapolis, MN, USA

Ben Rothke
Clifton, NJ, USA

ISBN-13 (pbk): 978-1-4842-9287-7
https://doi.org/10.1007/978-1-4842-9288-4

ISBN-13 (electronic): 978-1-4842-9288-4

Managing Director, Apress Media LLC: Welmoed Spahr
Acquisitions Editor: Susan McDermott
Development Editor: James Markham
Coordinating Editor: Jessica Vakili

Distributed to the book trade worldwide by Springer Science+Business Media New York, 233 Spring Street, 6th Floor, New York, NY 10013. Phone 1-800-SPRINGER, fax (201) 348-4505, e-mail orders-ny@springer-sbm.com, or visit www.springeronline.com. Apress Media, LLC is a California LLC and the sole member (owner) is Springer Science + Business Media Finance Inc (SSBM Finance Inc). SSBM Finance Inc is a **Delaware** corporation.

For information on translations, please e-mail booktranslations@springernature.com; for reprint, paperback, or audio rights, please e-mail bookpermissions@springernature.com.

Apress titles may be purchased in bulk for academic, corporate, or promotional use. eBook versions and licenses are also available for most titles. For more information, reference our Print and eBook Bulk Sales web page at http://www.apress.com/bulk-sales.

Any source code or other supplementary material referenced by the author in this book is available to readers on the Github repository: https://github.com/Apress/The-Definitive-Guide-to-PCI-DSS-Version-4. For more detailed information, please visit http://www.apress.com/source-code.

Printed on acid-free paper

Table of Contents

About the Authors

Arthur B. Cooper Jr. ("Coop") is a Principal Security Consultant at TrustedSec. He has 45 years of experience in information technology with the last 20 years focused on the security of payment systems and architectures, ecommerce, payment application assessments, forensic investigations, compliance security assessments, development of secure network architectures, risk management programs, security governance initiatives, and regulatory compliance. Coop was a member of the US Air Force (USAF) for most of his young adult life and had direct experience with the original ARPANET and ARPANET 1822 protocols. He was directly involved with the original DoD X.25 networks, the Defense Data Network (DDN), and the Automatic Digital Information Network (AUTODIN). He was directly involved with the original BBN Packet Switch Node (PSN) systems and has witnessed every major information technology "leap" or development since that time.

Coop was the standards trainer for the Payment Card Industry Security Standards Council (PCI SSC) for three years from 2010 to 2013 and has been a consultant to some of the largest retail companies and financial institutions in the world. He has worked with businesses to improve their overall security posture and to meet compliance regulations such as PCI, HIPAA, GLBA, and SOX. Coop is an experienced team leader and IT security expert who can ensure timely and successful completion of projects, as well as an enthusiastic security engineer researching emerging security technologies, trends, and tools. His certifications include Security+, CEH, CISA, CDPSE, CISSP, PCIP, and PCI QSA.

Jeff Hall is Principal Security Consultant at Truvantis, Inc. He has over 30 years of technology and compliance project experience. Jeff has done a significant amount of work with financial institutions and the healthcare, manufacturing, and distribution industries, including security assessments, strategic technology planning, and application implementation. He is part of the PCI Dream Team (DT) and is the writer of the PCI Guru blog, the definitive source for PCI DSS information.

David Mundhenk is Principal Security Consultant at the eDelta Consulting, as an information security, governance, risk, and compliance consultant with extensive multi-organizational experience providing a myriad of professional security services to business and government entities worldwide. He has worked as a computer and network system security professional for more than 30 years. David's experience covers a broad spectrum of security disciplines, including security compliance assessments, security product quality assurance, vulnerability scanning, penetration testing, application security assessments, network and host intrusion detection/prevention, disaster and recovery planning, protocol analysis, formal security training instruction, and social engineering. He has successfully completed 200+ PCI DSS assessments and scores of PA-DSS assessments. Certifications include CISSP, CISA, QSA, PCIP.

Ben Rothke, CISSP, CISM, CISA, is a New York City–based senior information security manager with Tapad and has over 20 years of industry experience in information system security and privacy. His areas of expertise are in risk management and mitigation, security and privacy regulatory issues, design and implementation of system security, encryption, cryptography, and security policy development. Ben is the author of the book *Computer Security: 20 Things Every Employee Should Know* and writes security and privacy book reviews for the RSA Conference blog and Security Management. He is a frequent speaker at industry conferences, such as RSA and MISTI, is a member of ASIS and InfraGard, and holds many security certifications, besides being an ISO 27001 lead auditor.

About the Technical Reviewer

Jeffrey Man is a respected information security advocate, advisor, evangelist, international speaker, keynoter, former host of "Security & Compliance Weekly," cohost on "Paul's Security Weekly," and Tribe of Hackers (TOH) contributor, including TOH Red Team, TOH Security Leaders, and TOH Blue Team, and he is currently serving in a consulting/ advisory role for Online Business Systems. He has over 40 years of experience working in all aspects of computer, network, and information security, including cryptography, risk management, vulnerability analysis, compliance assessment, forensic analysis, and penetration testing. He is a Certified NSA Cryptanalyst. He previously held security research, management, and product development roles with the National Security Agency (NSA), the DoD, and private-sector enterprises and was a founding member of the first penetration testing "red team" at NSA. For the past 27 years, he has been a pen tester, security architect, consultant, Qualified Security Assessor (QSA), and PCI SME, providing consulting and advisory services to many of the nation's best known companies.

Author Introductions

Arthur B. Cooper Jr. ("Coop")

First of all, let me thank Ben Rothke. It was Ben who actually pulled together four ragtag old farts to assemble what would become known as the PCI Dream Team: Ben, Jeff, Dave, and myself. Together we have participated in many town hall–based webinars called "PCI Dream Team: Ask Us Your Toughest Questions," many of which were captured for posterity by BrightTalk.

Ben has also been very patient with me, as I am probably THE greatest procrastinator on writing anything for this book. This is not due to me not caring. In fact, quite the opposite. I care greatly about payment card security, and I have devoted the past 20 years of my life to the cause.

If anyone had ever predicted this is where I'd end up, I would have laughed and rebuffed them immediately. At the tender age of 17, I convinced my mother to sign some documentation allowing me to become a member of the US Air Force (USAF). No need to go into it all, but suffice it to say payments and payment security didn't rank high on my list of reasons to join up. However, the idea of security as a "calling" came to me at that very tender age of 17 when I saw what we (the USAF) were trying to accomplish. Security of my country rang loud in my ears, and I was hooked, pole, line, and sinker.

Some injuries, a "capture" of sorts, and some other maladies forced my hand, and I found myself being trained to work in military telecommunication centers. I didn't want to do that; I wanted to be some kind of superhero. Alas, my fortunes aimed elsewhere. At first, it didn't seem too exciting to me working in a closed building with no windows, and

I questioned my purpose and contributions greatly. Thank God I had some great military supervisors over the years, for they led me to the "promised land" of maturity and wisdom.

Let's flash forward many years and several ladder steps in my career. Around late 2004, I heard about the PCI standards being created. I jumped into the PCI arena with both feet and my eyes wide open. I was also fortunate enough to work for the PCI Council for a few years as a trainer, and all of my time on this journey has been very enjoyable. Hopefully I have been of some help to all of my clients over the years. I still love being a PCI QSA, and I always try to do the best I can when ensuring a client's compliance validation is accurate and timely and keeps them out of the news. I have been very fortunate, as NONE of my clients have ever been breached when I was working with them, and I'd like to think I had a small part in that.

I have no plans of ever retiring, unless it becomes medically impossible for me to help folks with their compliance and security needs. I work for the best cybersecurity firm on earth, and I will remain here until they pry my hands from the keyboard.

It has always been my honor and privilege to work with Ben, Jeff, and Dave on the PCI Dream Team and also with the entire PCI community for all these years.

Jeff Hall
The Guru and PCI

I started into the world of Payment Card Industry (PCI) compliance before PCI was even an acronym. In Fall 2002, I was running the information security practice at what is now RSM US and got a call from a partner to handle an engagement called a Visa security review – what turned out to be a Visa Cardholder Information Security Program (CISP) for one of the largest ecommerce retailers at the time, Circuit City.

My experience with security, as my experience with compliance, has followed a long and surreptitious route. I had flirted with both off and on throughout my career – first at KPMG, where I worked on occasional SAS 70 audits and did the odd mainframe security assessment, to finally coming fully into information security at RSM US.

From that first Visa CISP assessment, there was a lull for about a year, and then CISP assessments were becoming more and more common. I had been replaced as the head of the information security practice and moved into developing this new CISP service.

In January 2006, I was sent out to Foster City, California, to attend Visa's Qualified Data Security Professional (QDSP) training and obtain that certification as Visa was now requiring that to continue conducting CISP assessments. It was shortly thereafter that the PCI Security Standards Council was formed, and everything from the Visa CISP to Mastercard's Site Data Protection (SDP) program was transferred to the Council and became the PCI DSS version 1 and the Approved Scanning Vendor (ASV) scanning program.

As I did more and more PCI engagements, I had a lot of clients tell me I should write a book on the subject as they would tell me I had answers that they could not get anywhere else. While writing a book sounded intriguing, I thought the new form of publishing called "blogging" was an easier way to write, and so I created the PCI Guru blog in February 2009.[1] Since then, for better or worse, people have called me the PCI Guru.

At that time, there were plenty of topics to be discussed. My idea was to write something at least once a week, and I was easily able to make that happen. I also caught a lot of heat calling it the PCI Guru blog. After all, who was I to think that I was a guru of anything, let alone PCI? But as I have found out over all these years, there is still no source of PCI information quite like my blog.

---

[1] https://pciguru.blog

That leads to the importance of this book. There have been numerous books written about PCI over the decade and a half that the PCI DSS has existed. What makes this book unique is that it is written by QSAs that have more than a decade each of experience in the subject matter.

We have encountered all sorts of issues in those years that had to be resolved, from a vendor that deleted their customers' vulnerability scans in a software update to a client that had their SIEM fail and lost all their log data, to an equipment vendor managing a client's network that turned out to be unsegmented when they claimed it was segmented.

Yes, we have the audacity to call ourselves the PCI Dream Team, but that is exactly what we are. We are QSAs that are possibly some of the best if not the best QSAs around. Are we perfect? Oh, certainly not, and every one of us would admit that we have all made mistakes in our years of conducting PCI assessments.

But we have also solved some of the messiest and most complicated problems PCI has thrown at QSAs. It is not unusual for other QSAs to reach out to each of us personally or through our email account looking for advice as they encounter something they have never seen before.

From that, we have shared our experiences so that the PCI community can learn from our mistakes and successes so that the community is not continuously reinventing the wheel. This book is a continuation of that service to the PCI community by providing guidance for PCI DSS version 4.

David Mundhenk

Historically speaking, a measurably significant number of data breaches have been caused by flaws in applications and by the hackers who attempted to exploit them. In addition, hackers and threat actors have repeatedly targeted payment applications including ecommerce sites and point-of-sale (POS) systems. They do so because that's where the money is. Payment card applications have been specifically targeted and attacked for more than two decades. This is why the major card brands have, and do still maintain, their own payment card security programs, in addition to supporting the PCI SSC and the PCI Data Security Standard (DSS).

I have worked in the payment card security space for more than 20 years now. I began working with payment card security first as an operational security engineer for the state of Texas, helping to ensure security and PCI DSS compliance of their state ecommerce portal and cardholder data environment (CDE).

Later, I moved on to work with IBM Security Services for seven years, first getting myself certified as a Visa Cardholder Information Security Program (CISP) assessor and then later as a PCI Qualified Security Assessor (QSA) and Payment Application QSA. Eventually I was selected to head up the IBM PA-QSA practice, which I led for six years.

From 2008 to 2010 and while still working for IBM, I was the sole QSA and PA-QSA for the world's largest payment processor. I traveled the globe at their request to help them assess their many different payment processing environments and applications.

I also helped them test and certify almost a dozen PA-DSS qualified applications from point-of-sale (POS) systems and ecommerce applications running on mid-range systems all the way up through tier 1 payment card switches that connected directly to the major payment card networks. It was almost like going to graduate school in payment card security.

I eventually left IBM to join Coalfire's Application Security team where I worked to test and certify all manner of application architectures, but with a special focus on PCI applications. It was there that I also got P2PE QSA and P2PE PA-QSA certified.

After leaving Coalfire I moved on to the Herjavec Group (HG) as a GRC team lead working on all things GRC but especially PCI DSS work. As of the writing of this book, I am currently working as the PCI practice lead for eDelta based in NYC.

I have also been publishing and copublishing online articles and papers related to cyber- and PCI security since 2007, many of which have been co-authored with my good friend and co-author of this book Ben Rothke. It was Ben who actually pulled together what would become known as the PCI Dream Team: Ben, Jeff, Coop, and myself. Together we have participated in many town hall–based webinars called "PCI Dream Team: Ask Us Your Toughest Questions," many of which were captured for posterity by BrightTalk.

I truly believe that payment card security has done more to raise cybersecurity awareness for the general public than any other cybersecurity standard I have worked with. After all, the majority of the public use payment cards in one form or another.

Many of us have gotten that dreaded letter from our banking institution informing us that our payment card account has been compromised. So most people fully understand how important this subject is because most of them use payment cards in one form or another.

One of my favorite sayings is "…a rising tide floats all boats." I often close our webinars with the premise that the PCI Dream Team is not four crusty old farts espousing the virtue of payment card security. The PCI Dream Team is really a "community" of folks including all of you who understand how important this subject is and do their part as well to help ensure payment card security is paramount and maintained at the highest levels of quality possible.

It has been my honor and privilege to work with Ben, Jeff, Coop, and all of you while we work together to help raise the tide of awareness for all.

Ben Rothke
My PCI Journey

In 2016, I was a senior security consultant with Nettitude, an information security consultancy. I had been a Qualified Security Assessor (QSA) for a few years and found that even as detailed and prescriptive as the PCI Data Security Standard (DSS) was, my clients still had many PCI questions.

I found that, too often, these clients would direct their PCI questions to their hardware or software vendors expecting an unbiased answer. As often is the case with vendors, they will push their own solutions, rather than look out for the customers' best interests.

Sometimes these clients would ask their security consultants or advisors – who, while having extensive information security experience, were not QSAs or lacked expertise in the payment space – for advice, and their suggestions would often not be in line with what the PCI DSS required. At the same time, their suggested answers were acceptable from an overall security perspective. By not answering relevant to the PCI DSS, these answers put clients in a PCI non-compliant state.

With such issues in mind, I thought it would be a good idea to get some experienced security PCI professionals together and answer PCI questions. We would do this unbiasedly, not pushing products or services of the firms we were working for.

I reached out to three of the smartest PCI professionals I knew and suggested we do a webinar, which was the start of the PCI Dream Team. The first iteration[2] of the PCI Dream Team consisted of authors David (whom I worked with previously on a PCI project for a large entertainment company) and Coop (who led my QSA training and, in my experience, is one of the best technical trainers ever), in addition to my Nettitude colleague at the time, Jim Seaman.

In 2017, the next and current iteration[3] of the PCI Dream Team bid adieu to Jim and welcomed author Jeff to the team, and we've been a band of PCI brothers since. Many people know Jeff via his PCI Guru blog.[4] It's not just the name of his blog; Jeff *really* is a PCI guru.

So why is this book necessary? There are several existing books about PCI in print, from *PCI DSS: An Integrated Data Security Standard Guide*

---

[2] www.brighttalk.com/webcast/288/207869
[3] www.brighttalk.com/webcast/288/245165
[4] https://pciguru.wordpress.com/

(Apress) by former Dream Team member Jim Seaman to *PCI Compliance: Understand and Implement Effective PCI Data Security Standard Compliance* (Syngress) by Branden Williams and Anton Chuvakin, the upcoming book by Branden *PCI Compliance: Understand and Implement Effective PCI Data Security Standard Compliance*, and more.

What is unique about this book is twofold. Here, we tell you exactly what you need to provide your QSA for *every* PCI requirement. Even though the PCI DSS is quite prescriptive (much more so than standards and regulations such as ISO 27001, HIPAA, GLBA, SOC 2, GDPR, and others), a merchant or service provider can often be left scratching their head not knowing precisely what they need to show their QSA during an audit.

Here, we detail what specific documents we, as QSAs, need to see to attest to your PCI compliance. No other reference has this documentation list the particular documentation requirements for every one of the over 400 requirements of PCI DSS version 4.

The second benefit of the book is that we bring real-world experience and unbiased advice to every page of the book. We are keeping theory to a minimum and focusing on the real-world scenarios that most merchants and service providers face in their quest to achieve and maintain PCI compliance.

We are not reinventing the wheel here, so we won't be sharing information that has already been printed, the objectives of PCI DSS compliance, or other information easily available on the PCI website. We could have easily made this into a 1,000-page reference, which would gather dust. But we'd rather have it be leaner and of value. Our book is meant for PCI practitioners, so we expect the readers to have a decent understanding of payment systems, the PCI DSS itself, and other things fundamental to PCI.

The authors have more than 50 years of combined PCI experience and 100 years of information security and risk management experience.

We have seen it all, been there, and done that. And we are sharing our combined knowledge with you, to make your PCI journey easier.

We hope you enjoy reading this book as much as we enjoyed writing it. In case we didn't answer your question here, feel free to email us at pcidreamteam@gmail.com.

Foreword

My father always told me that if you stick around long enough, you get to see some pretty amazing things. In the case of credit card security, he was 1,000% right. I was lucky enough to be in the data and network security business most of my career and even luckier to be loosely associated with the major credit card companies in that capacity early on. I was fortunate to play a very small part in the early days and proliferation of the PCI Security Standards Council and the promotion of most of the standards they created.

The authors of this book, Jeff, Coop, Dave, and Ben, on the PCI DSS have also collectively been associated with the security business, specifically these standards, for over 50 years. Like my dad said, you see some pretty amazing things if you stick around long enough and, more importantly, if you're paying attention!

The authors have been in the thick of it right from the beginning and have obviously been paying very close attention. They have seen the industry go from what a security expert might refer to as the wild wild west to one that has become the poster child for the saying that you "must bake security in from the beginning" on everything it does.

They not only know this standard and all of its iterations, but throughout the years, they have worked with it closely and helped vast amounts of companies secure their customers' credit card and personal data. They have been involved in the review of these standards and the implementation of them in every scenario you could possibly imagine.

They have watched how credit card data security has evolved and worked with the PCI DSS from its first version and through all of its iterations up to today's version 4.

The PCI SSC DSS was developed to encourage and enhance payment account data security and facilitate the broad adoption of consistent data security measures globally. It provides a baseline of technical and operational requirements designed to protect payment account data.

The updated PCI DSS v4.0, released in March 2022, continues that mission by ensuring the DSS continues to meet the security needs of the payments industry, adds flexibility to support different methodologies used to achieve security, and enhances validation methods and procedures. Security needs to be a continuous process, and adherence to the PCI DSS v4.0 helps make that possible.

So whether you're a merchant trying to protect your customers' credit card and personal data or a security person responsible for implementing and maintaining the PCI DSS in your organization, this book will help you understand and have the best possible chance of keeping your precious information safe and secure.

And to quote *Hill Street Blues* (look it up): Let's be safe out there, people.

Bob Russo
Former General Manager, PCI Security Standards Council

CHAPTER 1

A Brief History of PCI

Welcome to the PCI DSS

Most people think that PCI began with the formation of the PCI Security Standards Council (PCI SSC) back in 2006, but the roots of PCI, in fact, go back to the late 1990s.

With the advent of the Internet and the development of electronic commerce, the card brands (American Express, Discover, JCB, Mastercard, and Visa International) began to see breaches of cardholder data (CHD) from the very beginning. The first brand to enter the security domain was Visa, with the creation of its Cardholder Information Security Program (CISP) around 1999.

In those days, the CISP was just a set of glorified Excel spreadsheets with the security requirements defined along with their testing. One of the authors (Hall) did one of the first independent CISP assessments in 2002–2003 for the now defunct retailer Circuit City.

However, all that was examined at that time was their ecommerce operation, not their physical stores. A funny thing about that first assessment was that the Excel spreadsheet was full of comments explaining who the actual developer of that program was – Deloitte.

Not to be outdone, Mastercard came up with their Site Data Protection (SDP) program around 2001 or 2002. Its notable contribution to security was the periodic vulnerability scanning of online ecommerce assets and

© Arthur B. Cooper Jr., Jeff Hall, David Mundhenk, Ben Rothke 2023
A. B. Cooper Jr. et al., *The Definitive Guide to PCI DSS Version 4*,
https://doi.org/10.1007/978-1-4842-9288-4_1

the Approved Scanning Vendor (ASV) concept. American Express followed with their Data Security Operating Policy (DSOP), Discover entered the fray with the Discover Information Security and Compliance (DISC) program, and JCB came up with their Data Security Program.

As you can expect, retailers were not excited to have anywhere from three to five security programs to comply with by January 2004, and they were loudly clamoring for a solution. The problem was that the legal departments at the card brands viewed any consolidation of their security programs as a violation of antitrust and collusion laws in the United States. Regardless, everyone involved agreed that a solution needed to be found. The situation was further exacerbated in Spring 2004 when Visa decided to push their CISP into the brick-and-mortar realm as they started to see breaches move from the Internet into physical retail store environments.

Between 2004 and 2006, several changes were seen. To alleviate retailers' compliance heartburn, American Express decided in mid-2004 to accept a Visa CISP assessment for proof of compliance with their DSOP. That was followed by Mastercard and Discover in early 2005, acknowledging acceptance of a CISP report instead of their own, although Mastercard kept their online security program of vulnerability scanning in place.

At the beginning of 2006, Visa began its Qualified Data Security Professional (QDSP) certification program to address the inconsistencies in CISP assessments that were now performed mainly by consultants. Three sessions were held between January and April 2006 at Visa's headquarters in Foster City, California. It is worth noting that three of the authors (Cooper, Hall, and Mundhenk) are all holders of the rare QDSP certification.

Finally, in early 2006, the legal powers that be at the card brands came up with the concept of the PCI Security Standards Council (PCI SSC), or the Council. With the formation of the Council, the Visa CISP (now branded the PCI DSS v1.0) was adopted as the PCI DSS v1.1 with some minor changes.

Mastercard's SDP online assessment program became v1.0 of the Approved Scanning Vendor (ASV) program. QDSPs were grandfathered into the program as the first QSAs, with formal QSA training starting in 2007. And with that, the PCI DSS process was born. The final piece of the puzzle was the first PCI Community Meeting held in Toronto, Canada, in October 2007 for all QSAs and ASVs.

How We Got to Today's PCI DSS

The PCI DSS v1.0 was actually published by Visa for their QDSP training. It was PCI DSS v1.1 that was published by the PCI Council in September 2006. This version adopted the PCI SSC's logo and contained some updated language and testing from v1.0 that focused on the standard being under new ownership.

In October 2008, the Council issued v1.2 of the PCI DSS. One of the biggest changes in this release was the adoption of the term "assessment" vs. "audit" due to CPAs arguing that under state laws, only CPA firms could conduct an "audit." Other changes focused on increasing the scope of the assessment from an external perspective to a 360-degree look at the payment environment and anyone that had access to the cardholder data environment (CDE). The other major change was the reordering and renumbering of requirements, which caused issues for many QSAs.

July 2009 brought us v1.2.1, which was mostly editorial corrections but did provide for the first time an example of a filled-out compensating control worksheet, something that was desperately needed.

October 2010 gave us the first major revision of the PCI DSS. v2.0 of the DSS brought us separate documents for the Report on Compliance (ROC) and the Attestation of Compliance (AOC). This version also began the alignment of the DSS with other PCI standards that had been published such as the PIN Transaction Security (PTS) standard and the Payment Application Data Security Standard (PA-DSS). The version also brought a number of clarifications that explicitly called out technologies such as virtualization to ensure that all elements of the cardholder data environment were assessed. Also around this time, the PCI Council announced that they would begin publishing standards updates on a three-year schedule.

The publication of v2.0 of the PCI DSS also brought the start of the Assessor Quality Management (AQM) process. Up to this point, QSACs had been filling out Reports on Compliance and Self-Assessment Questionnaires with no guidance as to what the Council and card brands expected. As it occurs today, QSACs were required to turn over a sample of their v1.2.1 assessments to the Council for AQM review. What QSACs found unfair about the rollout of the process was that they were given the AQM assessment criteria after the fact. It was like taking a test on a subject matter you had never been given. The result was that almost every QSAC was placed into remediation over the next year. Worse, other QSACs took advantage of those in remediation and told prospective clients that QSACs in remediation could not perform their PCI assessments, which was not true. The Council took a lot of heat from QSACs for the first AQM assessments. The Council also had to repeatedly tell QSACs and the public that QSACs in remediation were still allowed to perform assessments. It was not a good time for the Council or the PCI DSS program.

Following their three-year standards update schedule, the Council issued v3.0 of the PCI DSS in August 2013. This update to the DSS was coordinated with the update to the PA-DSS. The biggest change with v3.0 was its focus on addressing the threats that organizations had encountered in the preceding three years. Another focus of this update was to even further clarify and explain what was expected of QSAs in assessing entities for PCI DSS compliance as the AQM program was still finding significant inconsistencies in assessments. Key areas identified by the Council for the changes in v3.0 were identified as

- A lack of education and awareness of securing payment card information

- Weak passwords and authentication mechanisms that were allowing payment card information to be breached

- The challenges of managing third parties that impacted payment card security

- Slow detection of breaches and malware

Sadly, even with the Council's focus on these issues, these are still challenges even today.

The next change to the PCI DSS was driven by a threat, not by the three-year release schedule. In Fall 2014, the POODLE vulnerability to Secure Sockets Layer (SSL) and early Transport Layer Security (TLS) protocols became an issue when the US National Institute of Standards and Technology (NIST) stated that SSL and early TLS were no longer considered secure. SSL and TLS were relied upon particularly to secure online payment card transactions, so having SSL and early TLS declared insecure was a major blow to organizations maintaining their PCI DSS compliance. On January 30, 2015, the PCI Council declared in that month's Assessor Newsletter that SSL was no longer considered strong cryptography. This notification was apparently missed by most QSAs, resulting in the largest readership ever of a post on the PCI Guru's blog when he pointed it out in his February 7, 2015, post.

With the publication of PCI DSS v3.1 in April 2015, the Council added early TLS to the SSL protocol that was no longer considered strong cryptography. In addition to this, the Council also clarified that sensitive authentication data (SAD) was no longer permitted to be stored after transaction authorization. A number of requirements were designated as only applying to service providers and not merchants.

The Council set a sunset date for the usage of SSL and early TLS for June 30, 2016, which soon was revised. One of the major issues with remediating SSL and early TLS by the 2016 date was that a lot of equipment had firmware that could not be updated and had to be replaced. However, due to vendor manufacturing backlogs, replacements could not be obtained by the 2016 date, so the Council was forced to extend the date to remove SSL/early TLS out to June 30, 2018, and allowed organizations to use compensating controls and other mitigations to manage the risk. Even after the 2018 deadline, organizations were still allowed to mitigate the risks as a lot of organizations, particularly those in Asia, still needed to support SSL and early TLS for their customers.

In April 2016, the Council issued another update to the PCI DSS with the release of v3.2. A year after the declaration that SSL and early TLS were no longer considered secure, the Council had to update the DSS to cover the issues discovered as a result of the SSL/early TLS sunset decision. One of the biggest changes to the DSS that was overshadowed by the SSL/early TLS changes was the addition of the Designated Entities Supplemental Validation (DESV) requirements as Appendix A3. The DESV had been a separate document up until this point. Another appendix, A2, was added to address the mitigation of SSL and early TLS.

Version 3.2.1 was released in May 2018. With the tumult caused by the SSL and early TLS threat, the Council abandoned the three-year schedule and basically stated that they would update the standards based on need to address threats, not a schedule. The bulk of this update was to remove the various 2018 effective dates from requirements since those dates had passed. Some additional guidance and clarifications were provided to further address QSA consistency in assessments.

This gets us to v4.0, which the Council published in March 2022. Version 4.0 is a total revamp of the PCI DSS and the reason behind this book. Requirements have been renumbered and regrouped so that they make better sense and the assessment flows better. A whole slew of new requirements have been added to focus on new threats, particularly those against service providers. The key issue though with everyone being assessed is the date it must be used, which is April 1, 2024. Any assessments started after that date must use v4.0.

One of the more controversial changes was the addition of "In Place with Remediation" as an assessment finding in the Report on Compliance (ROC). After a lot of discussion and consultation with participating organizations (PO), the Council announced in Fall 2022 that "In Place with Remediation" will be removed as an assessment finding and will be added as an appendix. The Council has stated that those changes to the PCI DSS will be published in Q1 2023.

PCI Is More Than Just the DSS

When people mention PCI, they are generally referring to the Payment Card Industry Data Security Standard (PCI DSS). While PCI now encompasses many standards, certifications, and compliance programs, this book will focus exclusively on the DSS.

But PCI is more than just the DSS. In fact, the Council has created additional standards to address other topics not directly addressed by the DSS. Each standard has its own certified assessors to conduct these assessments.

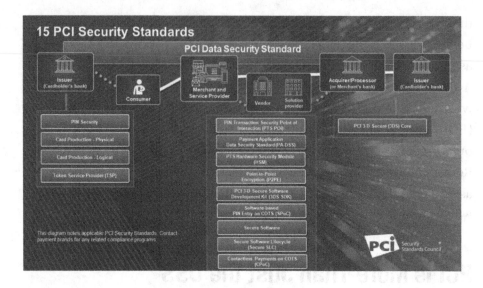

Some of the more notable of these include

Secure Software Standard[1]: Defines the security requirements and assessment procedures for software vendors of off-the-shelf payment applications. The Secure Software Standard replaced the Payment Application Data Security Standard (PA-DSS) in 2018. Secure Software Assessors conduct payment application assessments to validate that a payment application complies with the Secure Software Standard.

Secure SLC Standard[2]: Focused on the software development lifecycle (SDLC) process used to develop payment applications. This standard was primarily developed for organizations that develop bespoke payment processing applications, which are not eligible for Secure Software Standard assessments, but can be used by any organization that wants to develop secure applications. Secure SLC Assessors are only allowed to conduct these assessments.

---

[1] https://docs-prv.pcisecuritystandards.org/Software%20Security/
Standard/PCI-Secure-Software-Standard-v1_2.pdf

[2] https://docs-prv.pcisecuritystandards.org/Software%20Security/
Standard/PCI-Secure-SLC-Standard-v1_1.pdf

PIN Transaction Security (PTS)[3]: Provides information for vendors regarding the process of evaluation and approval by PCI SSC of payment security devices and reflects an alignment of the participating card payment brands to a standard set of

- Point-of-interaction (POI) and hardware security module (HSM) security requirements

- Testing methodologies

- Approval processes

PCI Point-to-Point Encryption (P2PE)[4]: Defines requirements to ensure secure encryption of payment card data and secure management of encryption and decryption devices.

PCI Card Production Logical Security Requirements and Physical Security Requirements[5]: Defines physical and logical security requirements for entities involved in card production and provisioning, which may include manufacturers, personalizers, pre-personalizers, chip embedders, data preparation, and fulfillment.

PCI Token Service Provider Security Requirements: Defines the additional security requirements and assessment procedures for token service providers (i.e., EMV payment tokens).

This is but a few of the other standards. The entire set of listings can be found on the PCI website.[6]

---

[3] https://listings.pcisecuritystandards.org/documents/PTS_Program_Guide_v1-8.pdf

[4] https://listings.pcisecuritystandards.org/documents/P2PE_Program_Guide_v2.0.pdf

[5] https://listings.pcisecuritystandards.org/documents/PCI_Card_Production_Physical_Security_Requirements_v2_Nov2016.pdf

[6] www.pcisecuritystandards.org/

9

PCI Version 4

The PCI Security Standards Council (PCI SSC) issued version 4 of the PCI Data Security Standard (PCI DSS) in March 2022. It replaced version 3.2.1 to address new and emerging threats and deal with newer technologies to ensure that PCI could deal with the many new threats against payment systems.

With 64 new requirements above what was in version 3.2.1, version 4 is a significant update. And it's important to note that while version 4 was released in 2022, the SSC has a transition period from March 2022 to March 2024 to give organizations the needed time to familiarize themselves with the many changes in the new version.

On March 31, 2024, PCI DSS v3.2.1 will be officially retired, and version 4 will be considered the active version.

There are a number of new requirements in version 4, which are considered *best practices* and must be in place by March 31, 2025.

The following diagram[7] details an overview of the planned transition timeline and potential timing for future-dated version 4 requirements:

PCI DSS v4.0 Transition Timeline*

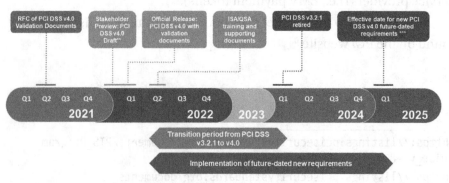

* All dates based on current projections and subject to change
** Preview available to Participating Organizations, QSAs, and ASVs
*** Effective date for future-dated requirements to be determined upon confirmation of all new requirements

---

[7] https://blog.pcisecuritystandards.org/updated-pci-dss-v4.0-timeline

And while 2024 and 2025 may seem like a way away, the changes needed to be compliant with version 4 take time to properly test and implement. And these deadlines have a way to suddenly appear much sooner than expected. Our advice: Your version 4 planning should be fully implemented ASAP.

CHAPTER 2

Install and Maintain Network Security Controls

The Payment Card Industry Data Security Standard (PCI DSS) was developed to encourage and enhance payment card account data security and facilitate the broad adoption of consistent data security measures globally. But it is important to understand that what is good for payment card account data security is good for any and every aspect of all data security.

Requirement 1 sets the foundation for solid payment card account data security. PCI version 4 introduces the term "network security controls" (NSCs), which is used over 60 times in the DSS. NSCs, such as firewalls with appropriate rules, load balancers also with appropriate rules, network switches with access control lists (ACLs), and other network security technologies, enforce network policies that are fundamental to information security and control of network traffic between logical or physical network segments.

© Arthur B. Cooper Jr., Jeff Hall, David Mundhenk, Ben Rothke 2023
A. B. Cooper Jr. et al., *The Definitive Guide to PCI DSS Version 4*,
https://doi.org/10.1007/978-1-4842-9288-4_2

Overview

It is hard to believe that people still do not fully understand the point of this requirement, and many people wonder why it has never been combined with "Requirement 2 – Apply Secure Configurations to All System Components." However, this requirement is separate because these devices are the first line of defense of a network and the proper management and control of network traffic is the first key step in securing a network.

The most significant change with v4 is the use of the term "NSCs" instead of the former firewalls and routers. The reason given by the Council is that firewalls and routers are not the only devices that can provide first-level network security. Although QSAs still encounter firewalls in most client environments, load balancers and other network devices are taking over the management of the network and its protection.

You still run into the occasional router, but that is becoming even rarer as organizations move into the cloud and containerize. Regardless of the technology used to establish network security, the concept of traffic management is the key, and that is what Requirement 1 is all about.

Evidence

To show that the organization is complying with this requirement, you will need to provide at least the following evidence:

- *Network management roles and responsibilities*: This is a document or set of documents that evidence that the organization has formally documented network administration roles and responsibilities. This can be provided in job descriptions for all positions involved, as well as it can be evidenced in a document that calls out the roles and responsibilities of the network administration team.

- *Network device configuration standards*: This is one or more documents that define the standards followed for configuring the network devices that protect the network, such as routers, firewalls, load balancers, and other network security devices that route network traffic. Typically, there is one document for every device type. These standards need to document the approved ports/services/protocols and be sufficiently documented to make the review of the configurations so that errors can be identified.

- *Network device configuration review procedures*: These procedures need to be sufficient to allow any network administrator to be able to conduct a review of all network security device configurations and identify that those devices are properly configured or, if there are errors in the configuration, the procedures to be followed and the time allowed for remediation.

- *Network diagrams*: These diagrams need to have sufficient detail to be used in the configuration review process to ensure that PCI scope is maintained. At a minimum, sufficient detail includes all network ingress/egress points, IP addresses for all networks on the diagrams, key network security devices, key servers, and data stores.

- *Data flow diagrams*: These diagrams need to document how sensitive authentication data (SAD) and/or cardholder data (CHD) flows across the network. This is important because it helps to define what is in scope for PCI compliance and what is out of scope. As Coop has always said, "Follow the data!" when determining PCI scope.

- *Network device vendor documentation*: This does not mean you have to print out manuals, but you need to provide your QSA with the PDFs or URLs for those manuals because not all that reference material is publicly available. As such, you need to ensure that materials that are not publicly available are provided to the QSA.

- *End user management tools and documentation*: When you have devices that can directly connect to the CDE, you need to have the capability to manage and control those devices to ensure that they cannot compromise or "infect" the systems in the CDE.

- Samples of error messages: The PCI DSS requires that you prove that error handling and error messages do not inadvertently display sensitive internal network information such as internal IP addresses, DNS names, NetBIOS names, and similar information that an attacker can use to compromise the environment.

Pitfalls

The most prominent pitfall organizations run into complying with these requirements is with the network and data flow diagrams. These diagrams are critical to giving your QSA an understanding of how your environment works and that you truly understand your scope for PCI compliance. The simplest mistake is not being able to prove that the diagrams are current and up to date. Although most people will point to a date on the diagram or the file date, that is incomplete. Diagrams need to have an update and/or review date documented as part of the diagram.

There needs to be evidence that the diagrams have been reviewed, typically evidenced by a work ticket or email message that discusses the review of the diagrams. Diagrams need to be reviewed at least annually or whenever significant changes have been made to the PCI in-scope environment. So put in a Jira ticket that is due every year and a flag in your Jira ticket to indicate that the change is significant so that you do not miss this one.

The other area where diagrams become an issue is that the data flow diagram is not overlaid on the network diagram. Coop taught at the PCI Council for several years, and his mantra there was "follow the data" when it came to determining PCI scope. If your data flow diagram does not overlay your network diagram, it is impossible to verify the scope, which is a job of the organization being assessed and the QSA. Therefore, do not be surprised to have your QSA reject your great-looking swimlane data flow diagram when it does not provide documentation of how that process flows over the network diagram. That is not to say that the swim lane diagram is not relavent and should not be included for clarification of how data flows in your environment, just that such a diagram does not facilitate following the data to ensure that an organization's PCI scope is accurate.

Device configuration standards have started to become an issue as firms move to the cloud and containerization. Many organizations point to the fact that the cloud provider or the container environment provides this security measure. Nothing could be further from the truth.

While the cloud or container provider provides a firewall capability and ensures that it is kept current, it is still the organization's responsibility to ensure that the firewall capability is properly configured and reviewed. As with a traditional firewall, this requires the creation of a configuration standard so that anyone given the task of reviewing the configuration can accurately determine if the standard is being followed.

Speaking of Network device configuration reviews, they are also becoming an issue now that organizations are in the cloud or using containers. The claim is that reviews cannot be performed because the configurations cannot be reviewed because of how they are now maintained or that they cannot be dumped out as in the past. Configurations can be dumped out, typically in XML or JSON format, and will take a bit of time to review because of that fact. Therefore, a tool is sometimes necessary for such a review to be more readily performed.

Speaking of reviews, the Council has gotten stricter with the management of time periods with v4. As with prior PCI DSS versions, the network security controls (NSC) rules are required to be reviewed every six months. And when the PCI DSS says "six months," it means six months give a few days either side of the actual six-month anniversary. As a result, it is essential that these reviews occur within the six-month window and there is documentation in the form of a Jira ticket or email that indicates that the review was performed, the findings of that review, actions taken to address any issues and the tickets generated.

Famous Fails

A favorite story about a failure in Requirement 1 occurred more than a decade ago. During the interview process, the network administrator confirmed, "We review our firewall rules semiannually." Then during the observation part of the assessment going through the firewall rules, the same individual said, "Oh, those rules. Those rules are for a vendor that we haven't done business with in three years." The QSA just could not contain themselves and said, "So, if you are reviewing the rules every six months, what are rules that have not been used in three years doing in the ruleset?" Sadly, this was obviously missed in previous reviews. Nothing says *non-compliant* more than admitting that you have old rules in your firewall configuration even though you claim you review those same rules every six months.

Another epic failure occurred a few years ago when a client moved from their co-location data center to the cloud. The QSA questioned the network administrator about the firewall that was in place between the co-lo and the cloud because it seemed to be missing on the network diagrams yet others on the staff continued to discuss such a device. This firewall was vital to keeping the segmentation of the out-of-scope devices truly out of scope.

After several rounds of discussion with all parties, it became clear that the firewall in question did not, in fact, exist – a fact that was soon confirmed by the penetration testing team, who found that the network segmentation was not in place. This is just another example of why the PCI DSS is structured so that such mistakes are picked up by one or more of the requirements and testing.

But possibly the worst failure ever encountered was when the PCI assessment was performed for a client while they were transitioning from an in-house data center to a new co-location data center. This move was supposed to have been completed by the time of the PCI assessment, but had not been completed. This was an organization that the lead QSA had been assessing for five years. A new QSA on the assessment team assigned to review the internal firewall rules came over and told the lead QSA that all of the internal firewall rules had been commented out. Baffled, the lead QSA went over to the new QSA's workstation and confirmed that all of the internal firewall rules were, in fact, commented out. After a number of urgent discussions with the client, they also finally confirmed that the internal firewall was no longer segmenting the internal network nor was it controlling network access to the cardholder data environment (CDE). A plan was rapidly put into place to address this glaring issue and bring the environment back into compliance.

Requirements and Evidence

1.1 Processes and mechanisms for installing and maintaining network security controls are defined and understood.

1.1.1 All security policies and operational procedures that are identified in Requirement 1 are
- Documented
- Kept up to date
- In use
- Known to all affected parties

- Information security policies that cover network security and related controls
- Network configuration procedures used to secure the CDE

1.1.2 Roles and responsibilities for performing activities in Requirement 1 are documented, assigned, and understood.

- Roles and responsibilities matrix for those who support the CDE and/ or have access to CHD, relevant to network security controls surrounding firewalls, routers, and other network security edge devices

1.2 Network security controls (NSCs) are configured and maintained.

1.2.1 Configuration standards for NSC rulesets are
- Defined
- Implemented
- Maintained

- CDE network hardening standards

1.2.2 All changes to network connections and to configurations of NSCs are approved and managed in accordance with the change control process defined in Requirement 6.5.1.

- Change management policy, standard, and processes

(*continued*)

1.2.3 An accurate network diagram(s) is maintained that shows all connections between the CDE and other networks, including any wireless networks.

- Network diagrams that detail the CDE

1.2.4 An accurate data flow diagram(s) is maintained that meets the following:
- Shows all account data flows across systems and networks
- Updated as needed upon changes to the environment

- Data flow diagrams that show the entire flow and lifecycle of SAD/CHD overlaying the network diagrams

1.2.5 All services, protocols, and ports allowed are identified and approved and have a defined business need.

- Comprehensive list of all ports/ services/protocols that are used inbound/outbound with the CDE

1.2.6 Security features are defined and implemented for all services, protocols, and ports that are in use and considered to be insecure, such that the risk is mitigated.

- Detailed rationale and management approval for the use of insecure protocols such as FTP, Telnet, etc.

1.2.7 Configurations of NSCs are reviewed at least once every six months to confirm they are relevant and effective.

- Evidence that network security controls have been reviewed and are reviewed every six months, including management signoff

1.2.8 Configuration files for NSCs are
- Secured from unauthorized access
- Kept consistent with active network configurations

- Configuration files for firewalls, routers, and other network security devices

(*continued*)

1.3 Network access to and from the cardholder data environment is restricted.

1.3.1 Inbound traffic to the CDE is restricted as follows:
- To only traffic that is necessary.
- All other traffic is specifically denied.

- Firewall ruleset showing how inbound traffic to the CDE is limited and restricted

1.3.2 Outbound traffic from the CDE is restricted as follows:
- To only traffic that is necessary.
- All other traffic is specifically denied.

- Firewall ruleset showing how outbound traffic from the CDE is limited and restricted

1.3.3 NSCs are installed between all wireless networks and the CDE, regardless of whether the wireless network is a CDE, such that
- All wireless traffic from wireless networks into the CDE is denied by default.
- Only wireless traffic with an authorized business purpose is allowed into the CDE.

- Wireless network diagram
- Evidence showing controls are in place to limit wireless access to/from and within the CDE

1.4 Network connections between trusted and untrusted networks are controlled.

1.4.1 NSCs are implemented between trusted and untrusted networks.

- Firewall ruleset showing how inbound traffic to the CDE is limited and restricted
- Firewall ruleset showing how outbound traffic from the CDE is limited and restricted

(continued)

1.4.2 Inbound traffic from untrusted networks to trusted networks is restricted to

- Communications with system components that are authorized to provide publicly accessible services, protocols, and ports.
- Stateful responses to communications initiated by system components in a trusted network.
- All other traffic is denied.

1.4.3 Anti-spoofing measures are implemented to detect and block forged source IP addresses from entering the trusted network.

1.4.4 System components that store cardholder data are not directly accessible from untrusted networks.

- Firewall ruleset showing how inbound traffic to the CDE is limited and restricted
- List of ports/services from all publicly available servers/containers inside the CDE
- Firewall or another security device documentation that states that network traffic ports/services/protocols that are not explicitly defined in rules are denied

- Security measures implemented to detect and block illegitimate traffic into the CDE

- List of all databases and their server/container IP addresses that store CHD
- List of ports/services/protocols from all publicly available servers/containers inside the CDE
- Firewall ruleset showing how inbound/outbound ports/services/protocols to/from the CDE are limited and restricted

(continued)

1.4.5 The disclosure of internal IP addresses and routing information is limited to only authorized parties.

- Documentation from network security devices that proves that they do not allow for error messages that display sensitive network information
- Samples of application error messages that prove that sensitive network information is not displayed in those messages

1.5 Risks to the CDE from computing devices that are able to connect to both untrusted networks and the CDE are mitigated.

1.5.1 Security controls are implemented on any computing devices, including company- and employee-owned devices, that connect to both untrusted networks (including the Internet) and the CDE as follows:

- Specific configuration settings are defined to prevent threats being introduced into the entity's network.
- Security controls are actively running.
- Security controls are not alterable by users of the computing devices unless specifically documented and authorized by management on a case-by-case basis for a limited period.

- End user device management, mobile device management (MDM), or similar tools configured to control the devices that can directly connect to the CDE
- Configurations for those end user management solutions that prove they are always running and cannot be modified or disabled by the end user
- Documentation regarding the conditions when management can have the end user management solutions disabled and for how long
- Details how administrators use VPN to access the CDE

Summary

The key to meeting the requirements in Requirement 1 all revolves around ensuring that there are adequate network controls implemented that will protect the cardholder data environment (CDE) and segment it away from other networks. These controls are backed up by certain controls in Requirement 10 that provide the ability to monitor these controls.

CHAPTER 3

Apply Secure Configurations to All System Components

Overview

While network security controls (NSCs) are discussed in Requirement 1, those NSCs and the rest of the systems and devices are covered in Requirement 2.

The entire point of this requirements section is to ensure that organizations are correctly configuring all their devices to ensure their security so that attackers cannot easily compromise them.

© Arthur B. Cooper Jr., Jeff Hall, David Mundhenk, Ben Rothke 2023
A. B. Cooper Jr. et al., *The Definitive Guide to PCI DSS Version 4*,
https://doi.org/10.1007/978-1-4842-9288-4_3

Evidence

In order to show that the organization is complying with this requirement, you will need to provide at least the following evidence:

- *Roles and responsibilities matrix – for personnel that configure in-scope devices and systems*: This is a document or documents that evidence that the organization has formally documented roles and responsibilities for configuring all systems and devices that are in scope for the PCI assessment. This can be provided in job descriptions for all positions involved, as well as evidenced in a document that calls out the roles and responsibilities of the team.

- *Secure configuration standards*: These are all the standards used to secure the devices and environments part of the assessment. These can be from vendors such as Microsoft, Cisco, VMware, Azure, Docker, Red Hat, Palo Alto, Oracle, AWS, Kubernetes, etc. These standards can be from a recognized security organization such as the Center for Internet Security (CIS) or the US Cybersecurity and Infrastructure Security Agency (CISA). They can even be in-house developed from all the aforementioned sources with organization customizations. The important thing to remember is that the standards must be formally documented and regularly updated.

- *Secure configuration standards update policies and procedures*: These are policies and procedures that document the conditions under which the security configuration standards and procedures are reviewed and updated.

- *Vendor documentation*: PDFs or URLs for all vendor documentation for the in-scope devices and systems.

- *Wireless network policies, standards, and procedures*: Wireless networking policies, standards, and procedures. This is only required if wireless networking is in scope for the assessment. And as a reminder, requirement 11.2 is always in scope whether wireless networking is in scope or not.

- *Wireless network configuration standards*: Secure configuration standards for wireless networks. This is only required if wireless networking is in scope for the assessment.

- *Wireless network configuration procedures*: Secure configuration procedures for wireless networks. This is only required if wireless networking is in scope for the assessment.

- *Business justifications for any insecure ports, services, or protocols in use*: When insecure ports, services, or protocols such as FTP, Telnet, etc. are used, the organization needs to provide a business justification for using these ports, services, or protocols.

- *Additional security measures implemented for the use of insecure ports, services, or protocols*: When insecure ports, services, or protocols are used, the organization needs to document the additional security measures that have been implemented to secure those insecure ports, services, or protocols.

- *Non-console administrative access standards and procedures*: Documented standards and procedures related to non-console administrative access to in-scope devices and systems. In the "good old days" this was typically controlled by a jump server or similar device. In today's cloud environments, this is accomplished by the cloud's management console.

Pitfalls

The biggest pitfall in this requirements section is a lack of specificity and the ability to confirm that devices and systems are securely configured. It is not unusual for QSAs to find that configuration standards are not detailed or, worse, are not current. But the bulk of the problem is that most organizations lack the evidence of build sheets, checklists, or something like those to prove that their devices and systems were built to the current relevant secure configuration standard. One potential way to address this situation is to use the CIS Benchmarks as a way to ensure the secure configuration of devices and systems and demonstrate compliance with the PCI DSS. But you need to apply those benchmarks periodically to all devices so that they are all secured to the standard the same.

After not having documentation to show that their systems are built to a secure configuration, the next most significant problem is finding inconsistencies with those builds. Using scripts to dump the necessary configuration information, a QSA must compare that information to the relevant secure configuration standard. The problem comes when the sampled systems of a given type, say Red Hat Enterprise Linux 8, have significant configuration differences and it becomes painfully apparent that the configuration standard is not consistently followed.

Another area that catches organizations flat-footed is the fact that almost all network infrastructure is in scope for their PCI assessment. While network segmentation can minimize scope, any networking person will implement all VLANs across all switches, firewalls, and other network infrastructure as a best practice because consistency ensures better security and a more reliable network when changes occur. As a result, that brings all that infrastructure into scope because, in theory, the network traffic can flow over all those devices even though the traffic should not flow that way due to routing and firewall rules. Such rules should address the situation, but a QSA must look at a sample of all devices to ensure that network traffic is correctly managed and blocked.

Another common mistake is that insecure protocols such as FTP or Telnet are in use and no additional security measures are implemented to protect those protocols. This situation typically results in a fire drill to address the use of the insecure protocols by removing them or implementing the necessary additional security measures. If this situation cannot be resolved, the organization has no choice but to implement a compensating control.

Most of the time, wireless networking is not in scope for PCI compliance. Organizations have done what it takes not to have wireless networks involved in anything with PCI. However, there are times when merchants need to use wireless for the Spring Garden Shop in the store parking lot or mobile cash registers within the store. These wireless implementations typically are just fine and very secure. But every now and then, QSAs encounter a merchant that implements wireless using WPA2 and a shared key or with other security issues and then must figure out a fix or implement a compensating control.

Famous Fails

The most famous fail was related to the POODLE vulnerability in 2015 that caused SSL and early TLS to be considered insecure protocols overnight. SSL and TLS are usually associated with securing external communications; however, they are also used to secure internal communications particularly when administrators need secure access to systems.

A significant number of vendors were using SSL to provide secure non-console communications for system administration. Unfortunately, these implementations of SSL were embedded in the systems' firmware and could not be updated, thus requiring replacement of the equipment to use TLS v1.1 or greater. To make matters worse, a number of vendors were suffering from significant manufacturing backlogs and therefore were unable to immediately replace systems affected by the SSL. In some cases, vendors were quoting organizations in years, not weeks or months, to get replacement equipment.

All of this resulted in the PCI Council to back off their original deadline to stop using SSL and early TLS from June 30, 2016, to June 30, 2018. Even then, the PCI Council still allowed SSL and early TLS to be used as long as the organization had appropriate mitigating controls in place, functioning and documented in a compensating control worksheet.

Requirements and Evidence

2.1 Processes and mechanisms for applying secure configurations to all system components are defined and understood.

2.1.1 All security policies and operational procedures that are identified in Requirement 2 are
- Documented
- Kept up to date
- In use
- Known to all affected parties

- Secure configuration policies, standards, and procedures

2.1.2 Roles and responsibilities for performing activities in Requirement 2 are documented, assigned, and understood.

- Roles and responsibilities matrix for personnel that configure in-scope devices and systems

(continued)

2.2 System components are configured and managed securely.

2.2.1 Configuration standards are developed, implemented, and maintained to

- Cover all system components
- Address all known security vulnerabilities
- Be consistent with industry-accepted system hardening standards or vendor hardening recommendations
- Be updated as new vulnerability issues are identified, as defined in Requirement 6.3.1
- Be applied when new systems are configured and verified as in place before or immediately after a system component is connected to a production environment

- Container configuration standards
- Container configuration procedures
- Network device configuration standards
- Network device configuration procedures
- Server configuration standards
- Server configuration procedures
- Virtualization configuration standards
- Virtualization configuration procedures
- Wireless network configuration standards
- Wireless network configuration procedures

2.2.2 Vendor default accounts are managed as follows:

- If the vendor default account(s) will be used, the default password is changed per Requirement 8.3.6.
- If the vendor default account(s) will not be used, the account is removed or disabled.

- Corporate security policy showing that vendor default accounts must be changed
- Evidence that vendor default accounts have been changed before an NSC has been allowed into the CDE

(continued)

2.2.3 Primary functions requiring different security levels are managed as follows:
- Only one primary function exists on a system component.

OR

- Primary functions with differing security levels that exist on the same system component are isolated from each other.

OR

- Primary functions with differing security levels on the same system component are all secured to the level required by the function with the highest security need.

- Container configuration standards
- Container configuration procedures
- Network device configuration standards
- Network device configuration procedures
- Server configuration standards
- Server configuration procedures
- Virtualization configuration standards
- Virtualization configuration procedures
- Wireless network configuration standards
- Wireless network configuration procedures

2.2.4 Only necessary services, protocols, daemons, and functions are enabled, and all unnecessary functionality is removed or disabled.

- Container configuration standards
- Container configuration procedures
- Network device configuration standards
- Network device configuration procedures
- Server configuration standards
- Server configuration procedures
- Virtualization configuration standards
- Virtualization configuration procedures
- Wireless network configuration standards
- Wireless network configuration procedures

(continued)

2.2.5 If any insecure services, protocols, or daemons are present • Business justification is documented. • Additional security features are documented and implemented that reduce the risk of using insecure services, protocols, or daemons.	• Business justifications for any insecure ports, services, or protocols in use • Additional security measures implemented for use of insecure ports, services, or protocols
2.2.6 System security parameters are configured to prevent misuse.	• Container configuration standards • Container configuration procedures • Network device configuration standards • Network device configuration procedures • Server configuration standards • Server configuration procedures • Virtualization configuration standards • Virtualization configuration procedures • Wireless network configuration standards • Wireless network configuration procedures
2.2.7 All non-console administrative access is encrypted using strong cryptography.	• Non-console administrative access standards and procedures

(continued)

2.3 Wireless environments are configured and managed securely.

2.3.1 For wireless environments connected to the CDE or transmitting account data, all wireless vendor defaults are changed at installation or are confirmed to be secure, including but not limited to

- Default wireless encryption keys
- Passwords on wireless access points (WAPs)
- SNMP defaults
- Any other security-related wireless vendor defaults

- Wireless network policies, standards, and procedures
- Wireless network configuration standards
- Wireless network configuration procedures
- Wireless network vendor documentation

2.3.2 For wireless environments connected to the CDE or transmitting account data, wireless encryption keys are changed as follows:

- Whenever personnel with knowledge of the key leave the company or the role for which the knowledge was necessary
- Whenever a key is suspected or known to be compromised

- Wireless network policies, standards, and procedures
- Wireless network configuration standards
- Wireless network configuration procedures

Summary

The key to complying with Requirement 2 are documented standards and procedures that ensure the secure and consistent configuration of all devices and systems involved in the processing, storage, and transmission of cardholder data.

CHAPTER 4

Protect Stored Account Data

Overview

This section of the PCI DSS is all about the protection of sensitive authentication data (SAD) and cardholder data (CHD). While much of this section is related to storing primary account numbers (PANs), it also discusses SAD because there are situations where SAD can be exposed during transaction processing.

Even in secure transaction processing situations, SAD or CHD can be briefly exposed in device memory before being encrypted, tokenized, or otherwise secured. Attackers have become much more sophisticated over the years and are taking advantage of those situations where SAD/CHD is even only briefly exposed.

Evidence

To show that the organization is complying with this requirement, you will need to provide at least the following evidence:

© Arthur B. Cooper Jr., Jeff Hall, David Mundhenk, Ben Rothke 2023
A. B. Cooper Jr. et al., *The Definitive Guide to PCI DSS Version 4*,
https://doi.org/10.1007/978-1-4842-9288-4_4

- *Roles and responsibilities matrix for personnel data management responsibilities*: This is a document or documents that evidence that the organization has formally documented roles and responsibilities for configuring databases and files that are in scope for the PCI assessment. This can be provided in job descriptions for all positions involved, as well as it can be evidenced in a document that calls out the roles and responsibilities of the team.

- *Business justification for sensitive authentication data (SAD) retention*: This is a document that discusses why an organization retains SAD. Some organizations such as payment card issuers and payment processors can have valid business justifications for the retention of SAD. But for merchants, there is no valid business justification for retaining SAD after a transaction is approved or declined.

- *Controls that restrict use of removable storage devices*: This document discusses the controls that have been implemented to restrict the use of any removable storage such as USB thumb drives, USB SSD/HDD, SD cards, magnetic tapes and similar removable storage devices.

- *Customer encryption key secure transmission procedures*: Organizations that share encryption keys with their customers need to have documentation of the procedures used to ensure the secure transmission of keys to the customer.

- *Data disposal policy and procedures*: The policies and procedures for the secure disposal of SAD and CHD. These procedures will also include secure digital deletion of SAD/CHD from storage devices.

- *Data retention policy and procedures*: The policies and procedures documenting the retention of CHD and the time period the information is retained.

- *Employee roles and responsibilities that can only view masked PANs*: Roles and responsibilities of employees that only have access to the masked PAN.

- *Employee roles and responsibilities that can view full PANs*: Roles and responsibilities of employees that have access to the full PAN. This documentation is for employees with access to bulk decrypted CHD, not cashiers or clerical personnel that only deal with PANs one at a time.

- *Encryption key custodian acknowledgment and signed agreements*: Involves a sample of the key custodian acknowledgment and signed agreements for all the organization's encryption key custodians.

- *Encryption key management architecture*: If your organization is storing PANs, you are now required to have a formally documented encryption key management architecture. This architecture must explain how it protects the keys used to encrypt PANs.

- *Encryption key management policy, standards, and procedures*: Policies, standards, and procedures for managing encryption keys.

- *Hashing vendor documentation*: While hashing is one way, the problem with hashing a PAN is that a PAN is only 15–19 numeric digits in length and therefore the hashing of the PAN is not necessarily as secure as people believe. Thus, under v4, QSAs are required to review vendor documentation regarding the hashing algorithms used.

- *Inventory of methods used to render PANs unreadable*: Not only is this for masking and truncation of PANs but also hashing and encryption of PANs. This also needs to document where these methods are used, such as files, databases, etc.

- *List of employees that can copy and/or relocate PANs*: This is an inventory of personnel that can copy or move PANs in systems. It can be by role of the personnel such as Senior Accountants or similar positions or it can list individuals by name.

- *PAN encryption procedures*: Documents the procedures followed to encrypt PANs in systems. If multiple methods are used, then all methods must be documented.

- *PAN hashing procedures*: Like the encryption procedures, this documents the procedures used to hash the PAN. If multiple methods are used, then all methods must be documented.

- *PAN masking policy and procedures*: Provides all the policies and procedures used for masking the PAN. If multiple methods are used, then all methods must be documented.

- *PAN tokenization policy and procedures*: Provides all policies and procedures used for tokenizing the PAN. If multiple methods are used, then all methods must be documented.

- *Whole-disk or partition encryption vendor documentation*: The documentation provided by entire-disk/partition encryption vendors.

- *Point-of-interaction (POI) vendor documentation*: Documentation provided by the POI (a.k.a. payment card terminal) vendors for each model of POI used.

- *Encryption, hashing, and tokenization vendor documentation*: Documentation provided by vendors of all encryption, hashing, and tokenization solutions used.

- *Sensitive authentication data (SAD) policy and procedures*: Policies and procedures addressing the processing and transmission of SAD. In the case of payment card issuers, this documentation must also cover the business justification for storage of SAD if it is stored.

- *Technical controls that prevent copying and/or relocation of PANs*: Documentation of processes or controls that prevent the copying or movement of PANs to locations other than those locations approved by the organization.

- *Transaction processing vendor documentation*: Documentation from all third parties that perform transaction processing for the organization. This should also include the third parties' PCI Attestation of Compliance (AOC).

Pitfalls

The biggest pitfall we see is merchants retaining PANs when there is no reason to retain PANs. None! With the advent of tokenization and reusable tokens, merchants have no reason to store PANs in any of their systems. With PCI DSS v4, the effort to be PCI compliant becomes even more significant for organizations that have not been able to get rid of PANs.

A lot of that impact is in this section of the ROC. If there is ever a reason to stop storing PANs, this section is the largest reason to stop storing PANs as the PCI Council has made this section even more onerous on organizations that store PANs.

Unfortunately for service providers and financial institutions directly involved in the transaction process, they have little they can do to minimize their PCI scope because, at a minimum, they process and transmit sensitive authentication data (SAD) or cardholder data (CHD), let alone may also store it. There are strategies to minimize PCI scope for these organizations, but they will never achieve the level of scope reduction of merchants who can reduce scope to the point of interaction (POI) with tokenization and point-to-point or end-to-end encryption. This is a significant point of frustration within these organizations as management typically desires significant scope reduction.

The result of this is that a large portion of a service provider's or financial institution's environment ends up in scope for PCI compliance because they cannot get rid of the SAD/CHD to significantly reduce scope because their business is the processing/transmission/storage of SAD/CHD, therefore the significant impact of v4 on their PCI assessment. PCI DSS v4 is likely to be highly impactful on their PCI assessment as well as their gathering of evidence of their compliance.

The next biggest issue we typically see is organizations that mistake masking for truncation and vice versa. The two terms are not interchangeable, and the Council has finally called that explicitly out with v4.

Masking involves the replacement of PAN digits with some character other than a number, such as an asterisk or an "X," on any printed materials such as receipts or reports. Some older payment applications store a masked PAN in place of the whole, cleartext PAN that they used to store. Where a masked PAN gets confused with a truncated PAN is that a masked PAN also needs to follow the rules of truncation but with the addition of the replacement character for all digits removed.

On the other hand, truncation is all about a limited number of digits stored in applications and databases. Originally, truncation only allowed the storage of the first six/last four digits of a PAN. However, there are new rules for truncation that the card brands published in 2022, so the old "first six/last four" rule is no longer the only way to truncate PANs. FAQ #1091, updated in June 2022, covers the new truncation rules by card brands.

PAN / BIN Length	Payment Brand	Acceptable PAN Truncation Formats
16-digit PAN (with either 6- or 8-digit BIN)	Discover JCB Mastercard UnionPay Visa	At least 4 digits removed. Maximum digits which may be retained: "First 8, any other 4"
15-digit PAN	American Express	At least 5 digits removed. Maximum digits which may be retained: "First 6, last 4"
<15-digit PAN	Discover	Maximum digits which may be retained: "First 6, any other 4"

There is also a post on the PCI Guru blog[1] regarding the new truncation rules and the issues they could potentially create.

---

[1] https://pciguru.wordpress.com/2021/12/19/updated-pan-truncation-faq/

Famous Fails

The most famous failure of all time was the Target breach. Target thought their in-house written point-of-sale (POS) solution was encrypting track data at the point of interaction (POI), not the POS PC. The misunderstanding was related to the version of open source software that was installed on their POS PCs.

There were two versions of the software available, one that allowed encrypted data from the POI to flow through the POS PC to the transaction processor and another version that received track data in cleartext from the POI and encrypted the data at the POS PC. Target believed that they were using the version that encrypted the data at the POI when, in fact, they were using the version that encrypted the data on the POS PC. Because the POS PC was the encryption point, the attackers could gather the customers' track data while it was in the POS PC's memory before it was encrypted.

Over the years, there have been several failures exposing hashed PANs because the first six/last four PANs were also stored in the same table or database. The reason this is possible is that since a PAN is only 15–19 numeric characters in length, the entropy of the hashing algorithm makes decrypting the hashed PAN from the first six/last four PAN a relatively simple exercise. This situation only gets worse with the latest card brand truncation rules where the card brands all have essentially different rules. The key here is that hashed PANs should never be stored within the same database as the truncated PANs.

Requirements and Evidence

3.1 Processes and mechanisms for protecting stored account data are defined and understood.

3.1.1 All security policies and operational procedures that are identified in Requirement 3 are

- Documented
- Kept up to date
- In use
- Known to all affected parties

- Business justification for sensitive authentication data (SAD) retention
- Controls that restrict use of removable storage devices
- Customer encryption key secure transmission procedures
- Data disposal policy and procedures
- Data retention policy and procedures
- Employee roles and responsibilities that can only view masked PANs
- Employee roles and responsibilities that can view full PANs
- Encryption key custodian acknowledgment and signed agreements
- Encryption key management architecture
- Encryption key management policy, standards, and procedures
- Hashing vendor documentation
- Inventory of methods used to render PANs unreadable
- List of employees that can copy and/or relocate PANs
- PAN encryption procedures
- PAN hashing procedures
- PAN masking policy and procedures

(continued)

- PAN tokenization policy and procedures
- Roles and responsibilities matrix for personnel data management responsibilities
- Whole-disk or partition encryption vendor documentation
- Point-of-interaction (POI) vendor documentation
- Encryption, hashing, and tokenization vendor documentation
- Sensitive authentication data (SAD) policy and procedures
- Technical controls that prevent copying and/or relocation of PANs
- Transaction processing vendor documentation

3.1.2 Roles and responsibilities for performing activities in Requirement 3 are documented, assigned, and understood.

- Roles and responsibilities matrix for personnel data management responsibilities

(continued)

3.2 Storage of account data is kept to a minimum.

3.2.1 Account data storage is kept to a minimum through implementation of data retention and disposal policies, procedures, and processes that include at least the following:

- Coverage for all locations of stored account data.
- Coverage for any sensitive authentication data (SAD) stored prior to completion of authorization. *This bullet is a best practice until its effective date; refer to the following Applicability Notes for details.*
- Limiting data storage amount and retention time to that which is required for legal or regulatory and/or business requirements.
- Specific retention requirements for stored account data that define length of retention period and include a documented business justification.

- General data retention policy
- CHD retention policy

(continued)

- Processes for secure deletion or rendering account data unrecoverable when no longer needed per the retention policy.
- A process for verifying, at least once every three months, that stored account data exceeding the defined retention period has been securely deleted or rendered unrecoverable.

3.3 Sensitive authentication data (SAD) is not stored after authorization.

3.3.1 SAD is not retained after authorization, even if encrypted. All sensitive authentication data received is rendered unrecoverable upon completion of the authorization process.

- Use a software tool to locate unencrypted payment card data in the CDE. The tool should be able to identify primary account numbers and magnetic stripe track data on stored computer systems, hard drives, and any attached storage devices.

3.3.1.1 The full contents of any track are not retained upon completion of the authorization process.

- Use a software tool as per 3.3.1.

3.3.1.2 The card verification code is not retained upon completion of the authorization process.

- Use a software tool as per 3.3.1.

(continued)

3.3.1.3 The personal identification number (PIN) and the PIN block are not retained upon completion of the authorization process.

- Use a software tool as per 3.3.1.

3.3.2 SAD that is stored electronically prior to completion of authorization is encrypted using strong cryptography.

- Screenshots showing encryption configuration

3.3.3 *Additional requirement for issuers and companies that support issuing services and store sensitive authentication data*: Any storage of sensitive authentication data is

- General data retention policy
- CHD retention policy

- Limited to that which is needed for a legitimate issuing business need and is secured.
- Encrypted using strong cryptography. This bullet is a best practice until its effective date; refer to the following Applicability Notes for details.

(continued)

49

3.4 Access to displays of full PANs and ability to copy cardholder data are restricted.

3.4.1 The PAN is masked when displayed (the BIN and last four digits are the maximum number of digits to be displayed), such that only personnel with a legitimate business need can see more than the BIN and last four digits of the PAN.

- Screenshots of display showing only last four digits displayed
- Access list of those who can view full PANs, with justification
- Evidence of management approval and justification for those who can view full PAN data

3.4.2 When using remote-access technologies, technical controls prevent copy and/or relocation of PANs for all personnel, except for those with documented, explicit authorization and a legitimate, defined business need.

- This is a new requirement that carries a high risk for non-compliance. Technical controls must be in place to prevent the copying or moving of PANs when using remote-access technologies.
- Access control lists for remote-access software
- Remote-access software configuration showing copy and/or relocation of PANs is prohibited by default

(continued)

3.5 The primary account number (PAN) is secured wherever it is stored.

3.5.1 The PAN is rendered unreadable anywhere it is stored by using any of the following approaches:

- One-way hashes based on strong cryptography of the entire PAN
- Truncation (hashing cannot be used to replace the truncated segment of the PAN)
- If hashed and truncated versions of the same PAN, or different truncation formats of the same PAN, are present in an environment, additional controls are in place such that the different versions cannot be correlated to reconstruct the original PAN:
- Index tokens
- Strong cryptography with associated key management processes and procedures

- Attempt to view the PAN via a text editor and ensure it is unreadable.
- Encryption key management architecture.
- Encryption key management policy, standards, and procedures.
- Hashing vendor documentation.
- Inventory of methods used to render PANs unreadable.

(continued)

3.5.1.1 Hashes used to render the PAN unreadable (per the first bullet of Requirement 3.5.1) are keyed cryptographic hashes of the entire PAN, with associated key management processes and procedures in accordance with Requirements 3.6 and 3.7.

- Attempt to view the PAN via a text editor and ensure it is unreadable.
- Encryption key management architecture.
- Encryption key management policy, standards, and procedures.
- Hashing vendor documentation.
- Inventory of methods used to render PANs unreadable.

3.5.1.2 If disk-level or partition-level encryption (rather than file-, column-, or field-level database encryption) is used to render PANs unreadable, it is implemented only as follows:

- On removable electronic media. OR
- If used for non-removable electronic media, the PAN is also rendered unreadable via another mechanism that meets Requirement 3.5.1.

- Attempt to view the PAN via a text editor and ensure it is unreadable.
- Encryption key management architecture.
- Encryption key management policy, standards, and procedures.
- Hashing vendor documentation.
- Inventory of methods used to render PANs unreadable.

(continued)

3.5.1.3 If disk-level or partition-level encryption is used (rather than file-, column-, or field-level database encryption) to render PANs unreadable, it is managed as follows:

- Logical access is managed separately and independently of native operating system authentication and access control mechanisms.
- Decryption keys are not associated with user accounts.
- Authentication factors (passwords, passphrases, or cryptographic keys) that allow access to unencrypted data are stored securely.

- Attempt to view the PAN via a text editor and ensure it is unreadable.
- Encryption key management architecture.
- Encryption key management policy, standards, and procedures.
- Hashing vendor documentation.
- Inventory of methods used to render PANs unreadable.

(continued)

3.6 Cryptographic keys used to protect stored account data are secured.

3.6.1 Procedures are defined and implemented to protect cryptographic keys used to protect stored account data against disclosure and misuse that include the following:

- Access to keys is restricted to the fewest number of custodians necessary.
- Key-encrypting keys are at least as strong as the data-encrypting keys they protect.
- Key-encrypting keys are stored separately from data-encrypting keys.
- Keys are stored securely in the fewest possible locations and forms.

- Encryption policies and processes
- Key management policies and processes

(continued)

3.6.1.1 *Additional requirement for service providers only:* A documented description of the cryptographic architecture is maintained that includes

- Details of all algorithms, protocols, and keys used for the protection of stored account data, including key strength and expiry date.
- Preventing the use of the same cryptographic keys in production and test environments. *This bullet is a best practice until its effective date; refer to the following Applicability Notes for details.*
- Description of the key usage for each key.
- Inventory of any hardware security modules (HSMs), key management systems (KMS), and other secure cryptographic devices (SCDs) used for key management, including type and location of devices, as outlined in Requirement 12.3.4.

- Encryption policies and processes
- Key management policies and processes

(continued)

3.6.1.2 Secret and private keys used to encrypt/decrypt stored account data are stored in one (or more) of the following forms at all times: • Encrypted with a key-encrypting key that is at least as strong as the data-encrypting key and that is stored separately from the data-encrypting key • Within a secure cryptographic device (SCD), such as a hardware security module (HSM) or PTS-approved point-of-interaction device • As at least two full-length key components or key shares, in accordance with an industry-accepted method	• Encryption policies and processes • Key management policies and processes
3.6.1.3 Access to cleartext cryptographic key components is restricted to the fewest number of custodians necessary.	• Encryption policies and processes • Key management policies and processes
3.6.1.4 Cryptographic keys are stored in the fewest possible locations.	• Encryption policies and processes • Key management policies and processes • Encryption key management architecture

(continued)

3.7 Where cryptography is used to protect stored account data, key management processes and procedures covering all aspects of the key lifecycle are defined and implemented.

3.7.1 Key management policies and procedures are implemented to include generation of strong cryptographic keys used to protect stored account data.	• Encryption policies and processes • Key management policies and processes
3.7.2 Key management policies and procedures are implemented to include secure distribution of cryptographic keys used to protect stored account data.	• Encryption policies and processes • Key management policies and processes
3.7.3 Key management policies and procedures are implemented to include secure storage of cryptographic keys used to protect stored account data.	• Encryption policies and processes • Key management policies and processes • Encryption key management architecture

(continued)

3.7.4 Key management policies and procedures are implemented for cryptographic key changes for keys that have reached the end of their cryptoperiod, as defined by the associated application vendor or key owner, and based on industry best practices and guidelines, including the following:

- A defined cryptoperiod for each key type in use
- A process for key changes at the end of the defined cryptoperiod

- Encryption policies and processes
- Key management policies and processes

(continued)

3.7.5 Key management policies procedures are implemented to include the retirement, replacement, or destruction of keys used to protect stored account data, as deemed necessary when

- The key has reached the end of its defined cryptoperiod.
- The integrity of the key has been weakened, including when personnel with knowledge of a cleartext key component leaves the company or the role for which the key component was known.
- The key is suspected or known to be compromised.

Retired or replaced keys are not used for encryption operations.

- Encryption policies and processes
- Key management policies and processes

3.7.6 Where manual cleartext cryptographic key management operations are performed by personnel, key management policies and procedures are implemented to include managing these operations using split knowledge and dual control.

- Encryption policies and processes
- Key management policies and processes
- Encryption key management architecture

(continued)

3.7.7 Key management policies and procedures are implemented to include the prevention of unauthorized substitution of cryptographic keys.	• Encryption policies and processes • Key management policies and processes
3.7.8 Key management policies and procedures are implemented to include that cryptographic key custodians formally acknowledge (in writing or electronically) that they understand and accept their key custodian responsibilities.	• Encryption policies and processes • Key management policies and processes
3.7.9 *Additional requirement for service providers only:* Where a service provider shares cryptographic keys with its customers for transmission or storage of account data, guidance on secure transmission, storage, and updating of such keys is documented and distributed to the service provider's customers.	• Encryption policies and processes • Key management policies and processes • Encryption key management architecture

Summary

The key concept for Requirement 3 is any organization that has access to a cleartext PAN is required to protect it regardless of whether or not they actually process it. That protection can take many forms, but if the entity is storing the PAN, they must encrypt it using strong keys and a strong algorithm.

The other key concept is that sensitive authentication data (SAD) cannot be retained after the processing of a transaction. But that is the key: the entity must be able to ascertain when a transaction is processed. For a merchant, this is easy as they generate the transaction. There are very few circumstances where this is not true such as with payment card issuers and digital wallets. But for any other organization, SAD cannot be retained under any circumstances.

CHAPTER 5

Protect Cardholder Data with Strong Cryptography During Transmission Over Open, Public Networks

Overview

Section 4 of the PCI DSS is all about securing sensitive authentication data (SAD) and cardholder data (CHD) when they are transmitted over public networks such as the Internet. However, the concepts presented here also apply to internal networks that are supposed to be not in scope for PCI compliance.

A. B. Cooper Jr. et al., *The Definitive Guide to PCI DSS Version 4*,
https://doi.org/10.1007/978-1-4842-9288-4_5

The definition of a *public network* according to the PCI SSC is any network that is

- Not controlled by the organization

- Accessible via public networks (this is most obviously the Internet but can even include multiprotocol label switching (MPLS))

Evidence

In order to show that the organization is complying with this requirement, you will need to provide at least the following evidence:

- *Roles and responsibilities matrix*: This is a document or documents that evidence that the organization has formally documented roles and responsibilities for managing and monitoring the secure transmission of cardholder data (CHD) over public networks. This can be provided in job descriptions for all positions involved, as well as it can be evidenced in a document that calls out the roles and responsibilities of the team.

- *Third-party/cloud provider responsibility matrix*: You need to have a responsibility matrix for every cloud provider or third party you rely on for PCI compliance. All of these entities need to provide a detailed matrix of PCI DSS requirements, including the description of whether responsibility for each individual control lies with them or their customers or whether responsibility is shared between both parties.[1] These third-party matrices should be compiled into a single document so that the organization can appropriately understand and implement controls to maintain PCI compliance between their organization and the third parties.

- *Secure data communication policy*: This is a policy that defines that all communications of PCI and other sensitive data over public or untrusted networks are required to be appropriately secured.

- *Secure data communication standards and procedures*: These are documentation that defines how secure communications will be conducted. Typically, these documents discuss the use of secure virtual private networks (VPN) or the use of TLS via HTTP.

- *Inventory of trusted encryption keys and secure certificates*: This is new to version 4, but many QSAs were asking for this documentation under v3.2.1. This is a spreadsheet or similar document that records every key or certificate managed by the organization used by secure communication protocols. This also includes self-signed certificates, which are now defined as acceptable.

---

[1] For example, see the *PCI DSS responsibility* matrix for Akamai customers and their Qualified Security Assessors (QSAs) for use in audits for PCI compliance. The responsibility matrix describes, in accordance with Requirement 12.8.5 and other requirements, the actions an Akamai customer must take to maintain its own PCI compliance when cardholder data (CHD) and other sensitive data are passing through or stored on Akamai's systems. www.akamai.com/site/en/documents/akamai/pci-dss-3.2-responsibility-matrix.pdf

- *Inventory of secure communication protocols*: Along with having an inventory of encryption keys and certificates, the organization needs to also track an inventory of the secure communication protocols used by the organization and their certificate expiration dates. The rationale behind this required documentation is the same as it is in Requirement 3, which is to enhance an organization's crypto-agility by documenting where encrypted communications are used, the protocols implemented, and when certificates expire.

- *End user messaging vendor documentation*: This is either PDFs or URLs for the end user messaging solutions used to transmit CHD.

Pitfalls

The biggest pitfall that is seen in this requirement is QSAs automatically accepting that an MPLS network is a private network. Unlike previous telecommunication solutions such as frame relay and ATM, MPLS is Internet Protocol (IP) aware.

The key here is that MPLS uses IP header information in order to route traffic properly. In essence, MPLS is no different from layer 3 IP switching/routing using VLANs on obviously a much larger scale.

The Council issued FAQ #1045[2] (*Is MPLS considered a private or public network when transmitting cardholder data?*) in 2014 about whether MPLS can be considered a private network. The bottom line from the Council is

---

[2]www.pcisecuritystandards.org/faq/articles/Frequently_Asked_Question/
Is-MPLS-considered-a-private-or-public-network-when-transmitting-
cardholder-data/

that a QSA cannot just accept the carrier's contract and assurances that an MPLS network is private.

The QSA needs to consider whether the MPLS circuit is shared and other characteristics in order to determine if it can be considered private. There are two blog posts on the subject as well that are worth considering:

- *The "MPLS Is a Private Network" Debate*: https:// pciguru.wordpress.com/2009/04/18/the-mpls-is-a- private-network-debate/

- *An Update on the MPLS Privacy Debate*: https:// pciguru.wordpress.com/2011/04/18/an-update-on- the-mpls-privacy-debate/

Another area that needs to be considered is whether the TLS certificates are appropriately configured and do not accept insecure protocols. The best way to test this is to use SSL Labs' Server Test website (www.ssllabs.com/ssltest/) to test the organization's TLS certificates. Not only will this site grade the certificates, but it will also tell you what protocols the certificates support. It is amazing how many times you will find that sites support insecure protocols as well as allow the use of TLS v1.0 and v1.1, which are considered early TLS by the Council.

The next significant issue QSAs end up dealing with in section 4 is the receipt of sensitive authentication data (SAD) or cardholder data (CHD) over end user messaging technologies such as email, facsimile, or SMS.

FAQ #1157[3] (*What should a merchant do if cardholder data is accidentally received via an unintended channel?*) was issued in 2012 and addressed the unrequested receipt of SAD/CHD via such technologies. The big concern for most organizations, of course, is that receipt of such information brings their email servers and other systems they have worked hard to keep out of scope now back in scope for their PCI assessment.

Do not panic. Such events do not bring these assets into scope if the organization is not encouraging their use in such a manner. That said, you can also not just let it happen and ignore the consequences. FAQ #1157 states that organizations need to take measures to ensure that such events are blocked with, say, the use of data loss prevention (DLP) technology. If that fails and the information still gets through, the organization must make sure that the information is securely handled and destroyed. Consider the title that Jeff Hall has given this: *the rule of incidental contact*. We have clients that politely write back to people that send their SAD/CHD to them via email and tell them that the channel is not appropriate for use and then delete the message. We have clients that, in the name of customer service, politely remind the customer that the channel is not secure but that they will process the request. They then conduct the transaction and then delete the message. The key here though is that as an organization you are consistently clear that sending SAD/CHD via the insecure messaging channel is not to be used.

A related issue is the use of end user messaging to transmit CHD. FAQ #1310[4] (*Are merchants allowed to request that cardholder data be provided over end user messaging technologies?*) was issued in 2014 and addressed sending CHD via end user messaging such as email and SMS.

---

[3] www.pcisecuritystandards.org/faq/articles/Frequently_Asked_Question/ What-should-a-merchant-do-if-cardholder-data-is-accidentally-received-via-an-unintended-channel/

[4] www.pcisecuritystandards.org/faq/articles/Frequently_Asked_Question/ Are-merchants-allowed-to-request-that-cardholder-data-be-provided-over-end-user-messaging-technologies/

The PCI DSS does not say that end user messaging cannot be used, but that it must be done securely. But FAQ #1310 reminds everyone of the huge caveat when end user messaging is used to transmit CHD, and that is the fact that the infrastructure used for messaging will be in scope for PCI compliance.

That means that email, SMS, and other servers used to provide end user messaging would have to be assessed under the PCI DSS. Since those systems would now be in the CDE, all systems that connect to those servers would also be in scope. Talk about scope creep! Therefore, any organization considering using end user messaging needs to examine why it is needed and then justify its use, as well as engineering the solution to minimize the scope impact.

An area of communication that does not garner compliance under this requirement, but needs to be included, is telephony over voice over IP (VoIP). QSAs and their clients ignore VoIP because it is not a well-understood technology because it is "the phone system." However, call centers conduct millions of payment transactions over VoIP circuits every day, and those communications occur over public, untrusted networks. Under Requirement 4, they also must be appropriately secured at least as far as the organization can secure them.

Famous Fails

The most famous failure of secure communications is from the card brands themselves. While the PCI DSS applies to any organization that processes, stores, or transmits SAD/CHD, it does not apply to the card brands. It has been widely known that the card brands violate the PCI DSS when they provide transaction data back to financial institutions, merchants, and service providers. It is not unusual to have such data transferred via FTP in the clear. This results in the recipient scrambling to ensure they secure these transmissions of data as soon as they are received. While the card brands have reduced the number of these insecure data transfers, there are still examples of them occurring even now after 15+ years of demanding such practices end for everyone else.

Requirements and Evidence

4.1 Processes and mechanisms for protecting cardholder data with strong cryptography during transmission over open, public networks are defined and documented.

4.1.1 All security policies and operational procedures that are identified in Requirement 4 are

- Documented
- Kept up to date
- In use
- Known to all affected parties

- Secure data communication policies, standards, and procedures
- Data retention policy

4.1.2 Roles and responsibilities for performing activities in Requirement 4 are documented, assigned, and understood.

- Roles and responsibilities matrix for those who support the CDE and/or have access to CHD, relevant to tasks for Requirement 4

(*continued*)

4.2 The PAN is protected with strong cryptography during transmission.

4.2.1 Strong cryptography and security protocols are implemented as follows to safeguard PANs during transmission over open, public networks:
- Only trusted keys and certificates are accepted.
- Certificates used to safeguard PANs during transmission over open, public networks are confirmed as valid and are not expired or revoked. *This bullet is a best practice until its effective date; refer to the following Applicability Notes for details.*
- The protocol in use supports only secure versions or configurations and does not support fallback to or use of insecure versions, algorithms, key sizes, or implementations.
- The encryption strength is appropriate for the encryption methodology in use.

- Inventory of secure communication protocols
- Inventory of trusted encryption keys and secure certificates used for data communications
- Reports from SSL Labs for all TLS certificates
- Screenshots of the payment processor console
- Evidence identifying and deleting stored data that has exceeded its specified retention period

4.2.1.1 An inventory of the entity's trusted keys and certificates used to protect PANs during transmission is maintained.

- Inventory of trusted encryption keys and secure certificates used for data communications

(continued)

71

4.2.1.2 Wireless networks transmitting PANs or connected to the CDE use industry best practices to implement strong cryptography for authentication and transmission.	• Inventory of secure communication protocols • Inventory of trusted encryption keys and secure certificates used for data communications
4.2.2 The PAN is secured with strong cryptography whenever it is sent via end user messaging technologies.	• Inventory of secure communication protocols • Inventory of trusted encryption keys and secure certificates used for data communications • End user messaging vendor documentation

Summary

The key takeaways from this requirement are that

- All communications of SAD or CHD must be secure, and this includes VoIP.

- Incidental contact with SAD or CHD does not immediately bring a communication system into scope as long as the organization is consistently clear that use of the system is not approved for such communication.

- All communication systems that securely transmit SAD or CHD are in scope for PCI compliance.

CHAPTER 6

Protect All Systems and Networks from Malicious Software

Overview

When the Brain virus was released in 1986, it was the first virus to attack IBM-based personal computers. It was easy to track down the two brothers who wrote it, as the virus code had their names and contact information in it: Amjad and Basit Alvi of Lahore, Pakistan.

As one of the first PC viruses, Brain was not destructive. That changed in the following years with destructive viruses such as Slammer, Code Red, Melissa, and many more.

Today, malicious software can do significant damage. From online attacks to credential stealing and more, malware is a serious threat that is not going away anytime soon.

Malicious software includes a wide swath of threat, from worms and viruses to trojan horses and more. Even if a payment application was built according to the PCI PA-DSS (Payment Application Data Security Standard), the underlying systems and workstation are still very vulnerable to malicious software attacks.

© Arthur B. Cooper Jr., Jeff Hall, David Mundhenk, Ben Rothke 2023
A. B. Cooper Jr. et al., *The Definitive Guide to PCI DSS Version 4*,
https://doi.org/10.1007/978-1-4842-9288-4_6

The main thing to do for compliance with Requirement 5 is to install anti-malware on all endpoints that will connect to the cardholder data environment (CDE) including all other systems/servers that are commonly affected by malicious software.

Up to PCI DSS version 3.2.1, Requirement 5.1 mandated to deploy antivirus software on all systems *commonly affected* by malicious software. Many took *commonly affected* to exclude the Apple Macintosh and Linux operating systems as they were believed to not be commonly affected by malware.

For the longest time, Macintosh users thought they didn't have to worry about viruses or malware, as most attackers focused on the more dominant Microsoft Windows operating system, as opposed to macOS. This was in exact opposition to the fact that the Macintosh was the first PC to have an anti-virus solution back in 1985.

For those using a Mac in a payment or merchant environment, there was long a mistaken belief that using a Mac meant they did not have to worry about PCI DSS Requirement 5.1.

What kept the Mac relatively safe was that the installed base was small compared with Windows and, therefore, not viewed by attackers as worthwhile to attack. But as the Mac became more and more mainstream and migrated to a Unix-like operating system with macOS X, it became just as susceptible to attack as Windows or Unix-based platforms.

The Shlayer trojan downloader,[1] targeted toward Macs, spreads via fake applications that hide its malicious code. Anyone using a Macintosh needs to pay particular attention to Shlayer. While it is an older piece of malware going back a few years, it made inroads again in early 2020 and still has not gone away.

Of the 12 PCI DSS requirements, much of Requirement 5 can be relatively easy, as many of the endpoints may already have anti-malware software installed. However, in the field, you may find that

---

[1] See *Shlayer: Destroying the myth that malware authors don't care about Macintosh.* https://medium.com/p/b68d77a33893

the point-of-sale systems (POSs) may not be fully compliant. What must be done is to ensure that anti-malware software is installed on all workstations and servers that are commonly affected by malware. This includes Windows, Macintosh, and most Linux systems.

The anti-malware software must be able to detect and protect against all types of malicious software.

The anti-malware software signatures must be updated regularly, and scans must be performed periodically. And logs of these activities have to be collected and stored according to PCI DSS Requirement 10.

One of the new requirements in PCI DSS version 4 is 5.4.1 This requires you to have processes and automated mechanisms in place to detect and protect personnel against not just malware but also phishing attacks.

While anti-phishing is a new requirement in version 4, it's hoped that most organizations will already have such controls in place. If they do, this is not that onerous of a task. For those who use an outsourced email service, your provider may already have these protections in place.

If not, a formal plan and process must be implemented to comply with this new requirement. The danger of phishing is that while you may have firewalls and encryption in place, all of that can be quickly put to shame by a single phishing attack.

When working on 5.4.1, consider another new control in 12.6.3.1 that deals with security awareness training that includes awareness of threats and vulnerabilities that could impact the security of the CDE. Phishing is obviously part of that. So ensure all of the requirements on 12.6.3.1 are considered when implementing 5.4.1.

Pitfalls

Most anti-malware software solutions are relatively easy to install and configure and run without minimal administration. And that can be the anti-malware software solutions' biggest pitfalls. As they are running on autopilot, errors can often go on for months without being noticed.

With that, it is imperative that all aspects of the anti-malware solution be regularly monitored to ensure that the protections that it affords are in effect.

Another potential pitfall that can derail your anti-malware software solution is if it is a cloud-delivered solution. If your staff does not have regular Internet connectivity, their endpoint will not have the most recent virus definition files or be running the most recent endpoint profiles. The final pitfall of anti-virus and anti-malware is not installing these solutions on servers as they, too, can also be commonly affected by malicious software. A lot of times administrators claim that servers' performance are adversely effected by anti-virus solutions. In some instances, this is true, however, that still does not abrogate the organization from protecting these systems and other mitigating controls must be used to address the risk.

The lack of connectivity will also affect inventory, configuration, and overall malware policy management.

Requirements and Evidence

5.1 Processes and mechanisms for protecting all systems and networks from malicious software are defined and understood.

5.1.1 All security policies and operational procedures that are identified in Requirement 5 are

- Documented
- Kept up to date
- In use
- Known to all affected parties

• Anti-malware policy

(continued)

5.1.2 Roles and responsibilities for performing activities in Requirement 5 are documented, assigned, and understood.	• Roles and responsibilities matrix for those who support the CDE and/ or have access to CHD, relevant to tasks for Requirement 5

5.2 Malicious software (malware) is prevented or detected and addressed.

5.2.1 An anti-malware solution(s) is deployed on all system components, except for those system components identified in periodic evaluations per Requirement 5.2.3 that concludes the system components are not at risk from malware.	• Evidence of anti-malware solution used
5.2.2 The deployed anti-malware solution(s) • Detects all known types of malware • Removes, blocks, or contains all known types of malware	• Evidence that the anti-malware solution in use has the necessary capabilities to protect the CDE
5.2.3 Any system components that are not at risk for malware are evaluated periodically to include the following: • A documented list of all system components not at risk for malware • Identification and evaluation of evolving malware threats for those system components • Confirmation whether such system components continue to not require anti-malware protection	• Detailed and defendable justification why the system components do not have anti-malware software loaded

(continued)

5.2.3.1 The frequency of periodic evaluations of system components identified as not at risk for malware is defined in the entity's targeted risk analysis, which is performed according to all elements specified in Requirement 12.3.1.

- This new requirement to define the frequency of periodic evaluations of system components not at risk for malware carries a high risk for non-compliance and must be adequately evaluated and addressed.
- Establish and document the review period for system components that are commonly at risk for malware.
- Show evidence of how the risk analysis was done to determine which components were identified as not at risk for malware.

5.3 Anti-malware mechanisms and processes are active, maintained, and monitored.

5.3.1 The anti-malware solution(s) is kept current via automatic updates.

- Screenshots of anti-malware solution admin console showing how mandatory updates are required for all endpoint devices
- Screenshots of anti-malware solution admin console showing how this functionality can't be disabled by end users

(continued)

5.3.2 The anti-malware solution(s)
- Performs periodic scans and active or real-time scans

OR
- Performs continuous behavioral analysis of systems or processes

- Screenshots of anti-malware solution admin console showing how periodic scans are required for all endpoint devices
- Screenshots of anti-malware solution admin console showing how this functionality can't be disabled by end users

5.3.2.1 If periodic malware scans are performed to meet Requirement 5.3.2, the frequency of scans is defined in the entity's targeted risk analysis, which is performed according to all elements specified in Requirement 12.3.1.

- Risk analysis showing how this was reviewed, defined, and approved by management

5.3.3 For removable electronic media, the anti-malware solution(s)
- Performs automatic scans of when the media is inserted, connected, or logically mounted

OR
- Performs continuous behavioral analysis of systems or processes when the media is inserted, connected, or logically mounted

- As this is a new requirement, ensure that the anti-malware solution is configured to scan for removable electronic media.
- Review the capabilities of your anti-malware software solution to ensure it meets 5.3.3.
- Screenshots of anti-malware solution admin console showing how removable media is automatically scanned for malware.

(continued)

| 5.3.5 Anti-malware mechanisms cannot be disabled or altered by users, unless specifically documented and authorized by management on a case-by-case basis for a limited time period. | • Screenshots of anti-malware solution admin console showing how end users cannot disable this functionality
• Screenshots of a sample of end users attempting to disable the anti-malware software loaded on their endpoint |

5.4 Anti-phishing mechanisms protect users against phishing attacks.

| 5.4.1 Processes and automated mechanisms are in place to detect and protect personnel against phishing attacks. | • Documented process of how end users are trained not to become victims of phishing attacks
• List of anti-phishing controls in place to protect staff |

CHAPTER 7

Develop and Maintain Secure Systems and Software

Overview/Intro

Statistically speaking, a significant number of data breaches have been caused by flaws in applications and by the hackers who attempted to exploit them. In addition, hackers and threat actors repeatedly target payment applications including ecommerce sites. They do so because that's where the money is. Payment card applications have been specifically targeted for two decades or more. This is why the major card brands have, and do still maintain, their own payment card security programs in addition to supporting the spirit and intent of the PCI SSC and the PCI Data Security Standard (DSS).

In this regard, section 6.x of the PCI DSS is regarded by some to be one of the most important sections of the standard. The PCI SSC has made some measurable changes to section 6.x as well as some significant clarifications. They have also made repeated references to "bespoke" software. Bespoke software is application code that has been created

© Arthur B. Cooper Jr., Jeff Hall, David Mundhenk, Ben Rothke 2023
A. B. Cooper Jr. et al., *The Definitive Guide to PCI DSS Version 4*,
https://doi.org/10.1007/978-1-4842-9288-4_7

to meet a specific customer's requirements. The PCI Secure Software Standard makes specific exceptions for software and applications that are created by a single entity, which is created to meet a single customer's needs. It is not marketed, sold, or supported for more than a single entity.

Here are the new requirements for 6.x:

6.1.2: Roles and responsibilities for performing activities in Requirement 6 are documented, assigned, and understood.

6.3.2: An inventory of bespoke and custom software and third-party software components incorporated into bespoke and custom software is maintained to facilitate vulnerability and patch management.

6.4.2: For public-facing web applications, an automated technical solution is deployed that continually detects and prevents web-based attacks, with at least the following:

- Is installed in front of public-facing web applications and is configured to detect and prevent web-based attacks

- Actively running and up to date as applicable

- Generating audit logs

- Configured to either block web-based attacks or generate an alert that is immediately investigated

One of the most interesting updates is Requirement 6.4.3 focused on the management of all payment page scripts that are loaded into and executed by a client-side web browser.

The client-side web browser attack surface has been completely overlooked as a threat landscape except by malware authors, the hacking community, social media, and mass marketers. All of these threat actors and business intelligence collectors continue to manipulate, and even exploit, end user client-side browser scripting vulnerabilities for ill-gotten gain and often under the guise of gathering "critical user business intelligence."

Traditional penetration testing and application security assessment tools, methods, and techniques tend to neglect this attack surface. They focus primarily on server-side vulnerabilities, not the client-side web browser. Thus "client-side" vulnerabilities are often referred to as the "Mariana Trench" of attack surfaces; they are very challenging to get to, and few have successfully addressed the issue.

PCI DSS v4.0 section 6.4.3 states the following:

All payment page scripts that are loaded and executed in the consumer's browser are managed as follows:

- A method is implemented to confirm that each script is authorized.

- A method is implemented to assure the integrity of each script.

- An inventory of all scripts is maintained with written justification as to why each is necessary.

This can be difficult to do; however, the Guidance section that accompanies this new requirement offers the following:

The integrity of scripts can be enforced by several different mechanisms including but not limited to

- Sub-resource integrity (SRI), which allows the consumer browser to validate that a script has not been tampered with

- A Content Security Policy (CSP), which limits the locations the consumer browser can load a script from and transmit account data to

- Proprietary script or tag management systems, which can prevent malicious script execution

The PCI Dream Team (DT) has been lobbying for something like this for some time now and commends the PCI SSC for finally addressing this issue with this new requirement. As a matter of fact, the PCI DT has also strongly urged the same protections be applied to payment redirection pages as well.

Requirements and Evidence

6.1 Processes and mechanisms for developing and maintaining secure systems and software are defined and understood.

6.1.1 All security policies and operational procedures that are identified in Requirement 6 are • Documented • Kept up to date • In use • Known to all affected parties	• Documented SDLC • Documented policies and procedures specified within section 6.x
6.1.2 Roles and responsibilities for performing activities in Requirement 6 are documented, assigned, and understood.	• Documented roles and responsibilities for all SDLC-related activities specified within section 6.x

(continued)

6.2 Bespoke and custom software are developed securely.

6.2.1 Bespoke and custom software are developed securely, as follows:
- Based on industry standards and/or best practices for secure development
- In accordance with PCI DSS (e.g., secure authentication and logging)
- Incorporating consideration of information security issues during each stage of the software development lifecycle

- Documented SDLC that contains requirements that all custom or bespoke software is developed based upon industry standards (such as OWASP), is done in accordance with all relevant PCI DSS requirements, and incorporates security issue remediation during each phase of the SDLC

6.2.2 Software development personnel working on bespoke and custom software are trained at least once every 12 months as follows:
- On software security relevant to their job function and development languages
- Including secure software design and secure coding techniques
- Including, if security testing tools are used, how to use the tools for detecting vulnerabilities in software

- Documented SDLC that mandates secure code training at least once every 12 months. The SDLC should also document that the training be relevant to their job function, include secure software design and coding techniques, and detail how security test tools will be used.

(*continued*)

6.2.3 Bespoke and custom software are reviewed prior to being released into production or to customers, to identify and correct potential coding vulnerabilities, as follows:

- Code reviews ensure code is developed according to secure coding guidelines.
- Code reviews look for both existing and emerging software vulnerabilities.
- Appropriate corrections are implemented prior to release.

- Documented SDLC that specifies that software be reviewed prior to being released into production and reviewed according to secure code guidelines, that code reviews look for existing and emerging software vulnerabilities, and that appropriate issue remediation be completed prior to production release

6.2.3.1 If manual code reviews are performed for bespoke and custom software prior to release to production, code changes are

- Reviewed by individuals other than the originating code author and who are knowledgeable about code review techniques and secure coding practices
- Reviewed and approved by management prior to release

- Documented SDLC that states if manual code reviews are being performed, they must be done by someone other than the originating author who is knowledgeable about secure coding practices and the reviews must be reviewed and approved by management prior to production release

(continued)

6.2.4 Software engineering techniques or other methods are defined and in use by software development personnel to prevent or mitigate common software attacks and related vulnerabilities in bespoke and custom software, including but not limited to the following:

- Injection attacks, including SQL, LDAP, XPath, or other command, parameter, object, fault, or injection-type flaws.
- Attacks on data and data structures, including attempts to manipulate buffers, pointers, input data, or shared data.
- Attacks on cryptography usage, including attempts to exploit weak, insecure, or inappropriate cryptographic implementations, algorithms, cipher suites, or modes of operation.
- Attacks on business logic, including attempts to abuse or bypass application features and functionalities through the manipulation of APIs, communication protocols and channels, client-side functionality, or other system/application functions and resources. This includes cross-site scripting (XSS) and cross-site request forgery (CSRF).

- Documented SDLC in which software engineering techniques are defined and in use to prevent and mitigate the software vulnerabilities defined within Requirement 6.2.4

(continued)

87

- Attacks on access control mechanisms, including attempts to bypass or abuse identification, authentication, or authorization mechanisms or attempts to exploit weaknesses in the implementation of such mechanisms.
- Attacks via any "high-risk" vulnerabilities identified in the vulnerability identification process, as defined in Requirement 6.3.1.

6.3 Security vulnerabilities are identified and addressed.

6.3.1 Security vulnerabilities are identified and managed as follows:

- New security vulnerabilities are identified using industry-recognized sources for security vulnerability information, including alerts from international and national computer emergency response teams (CERTs).
- Vulnerabilities are assigned a risk ranking based on industry best practices and consideration of potential impact.
- Risk rankings identify, at a minimum, all vulnerabilities considered to be a high risk or critical to the environment.
- Vulnerabilities for bespoke and custom and third-party software (e.g., operating systems and databases) are covered.

- A documented policy statement that new security vulnerabilities are identified using industry-recognized sources for security vulnerability information and that vulnerabilities are assigned a risk ranking based on industry best practices. Risk rankings identify, at a minimum, all vulnerabilities considered to be a high risk or critical, and vulnerabilities for bespoke and custom and third-party software are covered.

(continued)

6.3.2 An inventory of bespoke and custom software and third-party software components incorporated into bespoke and custom software is maintained to facilitate vulnerability and patch management.

- Detailed inventory documentation of third-party software components
- Critical software patching history

6.3.3 All system components are protected from known vulnerabilities by installing applicable security patches/updates as follows:

- Critical or high-security patches/updates (identified according to the risk ranking process at Requirement 6.3.1) are installed within one month of release.
- All other applicable security patches/updates are installed within an appropriate time frame as determined by the entity (e.g., within three months of release).

- Critical software patching history

(continued)

6.4 Public-facing web applications are protected against attacks.

6.4.1 For public-facing web applications, new threats and vulnerabilities are addressed on an ongoing basis, and these applications are protected against known attacks as follows:

- Reviewing public-facing web applications via manual or automated application vulnerability security assessment tools or methods as follows:
- At least once every 12 months and after significant changes.
- By an entity that specializes in application security.
- Including, at a minimum, all common software attacks in Requirement 6.2.4.
- All vulnerabilities are ranked in accordance with Requirement 6.3.1.
- All vulnerabilities are corrected.
- The application is re-evaluated after the corrections.

OR

- Installing an automated technical solution(s) that continually detects and prevents web-based attacks as follows:
- Installed in front of public-facing web applications to detect and prevent web-based attacks
- Actively running and up to date as applicable
- Generating audit logs
- Configured to either block web-based attacks or generate an alert that is immediately investigated

- Web application security vulnerability scanning and/or penetration testing reports

(continued)

6.4.2 For public-facing web applications, an automated technical solution is deployed that continually detects and prevents web-based attacks, with at least the following:

- Is installed in front of public-facing web applications and is configured to detect and prevent web-based attacks
- Actively running and up to date as applicable
- Generating audit logs
- Configured to either block web-based attacks or generate an alert that is immediately investigated

- IDS/IPS deep packet inspection firewall policy
- IDS/IPS deep packet inspection firewall configs
- Sample log files
- Screenshots of management interface including alerting on logs

6.4.3 All payment page scripts that are loaded and executed in the consumer's browser are managed as follows:

- A method is implemented to confirm that each script is authorized.
- A method is implemented to assure the integrity of each script.
- An inventory of all scripts is maintained with written justification as to why each is necessary

- Inventory of all scripts loaded onto payment pages
- Inventory of all scripts loaded to payment "redirection" pages
- Forensic evidence of testing of all scripts associated with payment and payment redirection pages

(continued)

6.5 Changes to all system components are managed securely.

6.5.1 Changes to all system components in the production environment are made according to established procedures that include the following:

- Reason for, and description of, the change.
- Documentation of security impact.
- Documented change approval by authorized parties.
- Testing to verify that the change does not adversely impact system security.
- For bespoke and custom software changes, all updates are tested for compliance with Requirement 6.2.4 before being deployed into production.
- Procedures to address failures and return to a secure state.

- Change control policy that addresses every requirement in this section
- Sample change control documents that demonstrate policy is being applied appropriately

6.5.2 Upon completion of a significant change, all applicable PCI DSS requirements are confirmed to be in place on all new or changed systems and networks, and documentation is updated as applicable.

- Sample of at least five change control tickets/workflows that demonstrate this

6.5.3 Pre-production environments are separated from production environments, and the separation is enforced with access controls.

- Sample logical drawings of the CDE and all boundary networks
- Penetration testing reports validating optimal segmentation

(continued)

6.5.4 Roles and functions are separated between production and pre-production environments to provide accountability such that only reviewed and approved changes are deployed.

- SDLC policy documentation that validates that roles and functions are separated between production and pre-production environments to provide accountability

6.5.5 Live PANs are not used in pre-production environments, except where those environments are included in the CDE and protected in accordance with all applicable PCI DSS requirements.

- SDLC policy documentation that validates that live PANs are not used in pre-production environments

6.5.6 Test data and test accounts are removed from system components before the system goes into production.

- SDLC policy documentation that validates that test data and accounts are removed prior to introduction into production environments

Restrict Access to System Components and Cardholder Data by Business Need to Know

Overview

This requirement isn't exciting when you first look at it. The title is long, and it seems to be something that common sense would dictate anyway, right? I mean, why wouldn't you restrict access from everyone with "no need to know"? Unfortunately, as we all know, common sense isn't very common, and any QSA who hasn't stumbled upon access problems when performing a PCI assessment is simply pretending. If you read about the many breaches we hear about on the daily news, there is always a consistent underlying theme. The attackers "gained access" to...

This then begs the question: how were they able to gain this unauthorized access? Most of the time it can be chalked up to a vulnerability that hasn't been patched yet, or many times it can be a result of misconfigurations within the various access control systems in place at the target entity. Even "script kiddies" can find these things with little or no effort, so it behooves us all to take access control very seriously.

Two Important Concepts

In order to fully grasp the intent of Requirement 7, there are two concepts of access control that must be understood:

- *Need to Know*: This is very important, because it may sometimes be subjective in nature. In the military, before one could gain access to sensitive classified information, three criteria had to be met. First, proper identification (WHO are you) had to be made. Second, did the individual have a security clearance commensurate with or higher than the classification of the information being accessed? Third, did the individual have a need to know? Only after all three of these criteria were met could one gain access. As you can picture, this made for uncomfortable situations when one's grade or rank was used in an attempt to access something they had no need to know about. In payment security, we define need to know as simply providing access to an individual based on the least amount of data needed to perform something or access something within the parameters of their job role. In other words, ask the question: "Does this individual

NEED to see or access this data to perform their job?"
If the answer is no, then the individual indeed has NO
need to know.

- *Least privilege*: This concept applies more to actions
  of access instead of applying to the actual data being
  accessed. In any security model, the best way to
  configure it from the start is to deny ALL access from
  ALL individuals. Naturally, you don't want to lock
  yourself out before you configure your own access (if
  you're the administrator of the system), but initially
  the person setting up the system should be the only
  person with the "privilege" of being able to access it.
  Think of setting up a firewall. Initially, you want the
  firewall to block everything until you open up the
  authorized ports, protocols, and services needed to
  conduct business. This is what least privilege looks like
  in action.

The Concepts in Use

Now that you have some idea of what these concepts mean, let us apply
them to PCI and payment card security. Within any organization that deals
with payment card data, management needs to decide what job roles apply
within every aspect and function of the organization. Each job role has to
be further refined to detail and document the data one will need access to
in order to perform said job. For example, how about a cashier working in
a grocery store. One could argue this individual will have access to several
credit cards throughout the work shift. But is that really true? Nowadays,
most grocery stores have payment devices that need no interaction with
the cashier when you pay with a payment card.

In the rare case that a card fails to work in the payment device, perhaps the cashier will have to assist or even enter the payment card number into the cash register or till. But does this mean that the job of the cashier requires access to any payment card data? Naturally, the answer is no. How about a bank teller? Perhaps this position requires access to any payment card data. Again, the answer is no. In both of these situations, limited access to payment card data is needed, but it needs to be defined. In the case of the cashier, it's access to one payment card at a time – payment device failures, assistance to an elderly or disabled customer, etc. are the only times access to payment card data should be authorized for that job role.

The bank teller may need access to payment card data if the customer they are dealing with has a situation involving a payment card, but again, this doesn't mean a bank teller deserves unfettered access to any or all payment card data. See the pattern here? Every job role in organizations that deal with payment card data will fall on a scale of needing access to payment card data. The scale will range from access to no payment card data all the way up to access to all payment card data within the control of the organization. In most cases, the only individuals with access to all payment card data at an organization are database administrators who actually manage the databases housing the payment card data.

It's easy to apply these two concepts of need to know and least privilege when you think of them both in terms of the job roles held by individuals who deal with payment card data. Does a cashier have any need to know every payment card number in the grocery store's databases? Obviously the answer is no, so now we can apply least privilege, which dictates the cashier's roles are restricted to dealing with one payment card number at a time, and this only happens when a patron has difficulty using the payment device, the payment terminal used in all transactions fails and card numbers must be entered manually, etc.

All-Encompassing View

When assessing an organization's adherence to Requirement 7, one must take a holistic view of all components within the cardholder data environment (CDE) considered to be in scope of PCI compliance. Every component needs to be examined in order to assure the access control system used by the component exists in a default "Deny All" state. In today's modern information processing arena, very rarely will one find a device or component that uses a default "Allow All" in the access control system. Whether a component is physical or cloud based, an access control system that starts up with a default "Allow All" access system would not be useful or secure.

Within the payment card community, one could see where any component allowing everyone access by default wouldn't be very useful or safe to use. In fact, it would be a nightmare to have such a device or component within the in-scope CDE. Unfortunately, there are some systems where a default "Allow All" access control system may exist. Perhaps it's a server running homegrown applications, and the applications are not configured to restrict anyone. Maybe it's a purpose-built device that only performs one function, but is connected to the network. Many of these devices are built with wide-open access.

This is why EVERY component within the CDE must be considered when it comes to access control. It is not uncommon for hackers to use printers and other devices to gain access to a network and then use this access to further escalate access to other devices on the network. As you can see, this is a real situation in many environments. Once again, any assessment of an entity's CDE has to include ALL components considered in scope of PCI.

Let's make a statement on what "in scope" means. Being in scope means the component stores, processes, or transmits payment card data. Then there is also the concept of "connected to" within the realm of PCI scoping. Basically, even if a device or component doesn't store, process, or transmit payment card data, it could be in scope. If the device or component is outside of the local network or network segment but still has some ability to connect to the same network housing the components that store, process, or transmit payment card data, this so-called connected-to device is also in scope. In summary here, ALL devices, components, systems, etc. considered in scope MUST be evaluated as to the access control system used.

Access Control Model

Each component must first be evaluated to ensure the access control system used by the component is indeed a default "Deny All" system. For example, servers running Windows, Linux, HP-UX, UNIX, or any other modern operating system are considered to use a default "Deny All" access system. Why? Because in order to access these servers, the operating system requires the assignment of a user account accompanied by user permissions in order for one to gain access.

Most organizations only think of components as hardware or cloud-based server instances. In the PCI world, this is not true at all. The various applications used on the servers are also considered components. A database residing on a server is a component. The small payment terminal where the payment card is swiped, dipped, inserted, etc. and doesn't even really afford any other access in the traditional sense is also considered a component.

Once ALL components have been identified, an access control model for the organization must be demonstrated to be in place. The model must include the definition of every role and the needs of every role with regard to access. Any access control model can be used, but in order to be compliant with Requirement 7, the model must be defined and grant access depending on the following:

1. The entity's business and access needs.

2. Access to components and data is based on job role classification and functionality.

3. Least privileges required to perform the job function are enforced.

All roles and responsibilities used in the access control model must be approved by authorized management personnel or those personnel delegated by management to perform such approval.

The model must be fully documented, known to all individuals within the entity's business operations, all activities assigned properly to individuals based on their job or role, and all assigned individuals must fully understand the organization's access control model and their place within it. It is very important that everyone within the organization understands what their job entails and what is needed to perform their job.

Maintaining Control

Once an organization has chosen an access control model, defined all job roles and responsibilities, assigned access based on said roles, and put the model into use, there is a need to constantly maintain the system as defined and intended to function. Larger organizations will need to review access privileges, system accounts, application accounts, and database access on a more frequent basis.

"Why?" you ask. Well, for starters, there are many more people assigned to large organizations, many more people potentially allowed to access payment card data, and many more situations where collusion between two or more individuals could occur resulting in unauthorized access to payment card data. Certainly a large payment transaction gateway or processor where there may be millions of payment card numbers in their databases falls into this category.

On the opposite end of this spectrum, there may be a small business selling ice-cream cones, and they are using a self-contained payment system where there really isn't access to any payment card data at all beyond assisting a customer to use the payment device. This is why reviewing access privileges at the ice-cream cone company could potentially be made whenever an employee is hired or fired, for example. This frequency of review would work well in most cases, as there is generally a new employee hired within each six-month block of time. User accounts and third-party/vendor accounts must be reviewed at least once every six months.

However, the frequency of review for application and system accounts must be based on a targeted risk assessment performed in accordance with PCI DSS Requirement 12.3.1. This is due to the fact larger organizations must perform this task more often based on the level of risk inherent to the business.

Keys to the Kingdom

Any hacker trying to breach an entity's environment is seeking the so-called keys to the kingdom. In the case of payment card data, any large repository of payment card data represents this "kingdom." This brings us to the subject of accessing systems that store payment card data. QSA personnel will always tell their clients to never store any payment card data they DO NOT NEED. Unfortunately, if an organization is involved with payment transaction processing as a gateway, card issuer, etc., their very business model involves the storage of payment card data.

These storage areas containing stored payment card data must be protected from general access, and if there must be access to the data, the access should be via an application or program where the individual gaining access can only perform actions enforced by programmatic methods. In other words, the application or program used enforces all access and actions based on user roles and least privileges. For example, a teller in a bank uses an application that provides access to a customer's payment card number, but will only allow the teller to access a single payment card number at a time. This is due to the fact the application has been configured according to the bank's defined teller role, and as we discussed earlier, tellers generally need to access payment card data on a limited basis, hence this role definition of viewing one payment card at a time. When the teller logs into the application, the application enforces this access control based on the user's privileges as defined in the teller role.

Are there situations where an individual's job role would entail access to every payment card number in a database, flat file, etc.? Yes, this could indeed be true. What about the personnel who actually administrate the database, flat file repository, etc.? Obviously, these individuals will be assigned a job role where such access is allowed. These individuals may need direct, non-programmatic access, but the important thing to remember is this access must ONLY be given to those individuals who are assigned a job role where such access has been defined, documented, approved, and implemented.

This is why in order to assess an entity's adherence to Requirement 7, the entire picture must be understood and reviewed. Ask yourself all these questions:

- What is the access control model used?

- Does every in-scope component have a default "Deny All" access control system?

- Are all job roles fully defined?

- Are all users assigned one of these job roles?

- Is all assignment of access approved by the appropriate manager or another delegated authority?

- Is all access fully documented from "cradle to grave," for example, initial assignment through revocation of access due to leaving the job or job role?

- Do all users fully understand the access required for their job or role?

- Is access being reviewed and maintained based on the frequency defined in the entity's targeted risk analysis?

- Is management ensuring all access is approved, reviewed, and accurate at all times?

Only after being able to answer all of these questions and have a holistic view of an entity's access control systems and their correct implementation can one fully validate compliance with Requirement 7.

Requirements and Evidence

7.1 Processes and mechanisms for restricting access to system components and cardholder data by business need to know are defined and understood.

7.1.1 All security policies and operational procedures that are identified in Requirement 7 are • Documented • Kept up to date • In use • Known to all affected parties	• Documented policies and procedures specified within section 7.x
7.1.2 Roles and responsibilities for performing activities in Requirement 7 are documented, assigned, and understood.	• Documented job roles, responsibilities, and levels of access assigned to each role, especially to access any stored payment card data

(continued)

7.2 Access to system components and data is appropriately defined and assigned.

7.2.1 An access control model is defined and includes granting access as follows:
- Appropriate access depending on the entity's business and access needs
- Access to system components and data resources that is based on users' job classification and functions
- The least privileges required (e.g., user, administrator) to perform a job function

- Documented access control model that encompasses all access to payment card data. The model must be based on the concepts and principles of "need to know" and "least privileges."
- Documented access control system specifications for every in-scope component.

7.2.2 Access is assigned to users, including privileged users, based on
- Job classification and function
- Least privileges necessary to perform job responsibilities

- Documented access assignment procedures
- Artifacts of access control system configurations, for example, screenshots of the Active Directory system, screenshot of an LDAP system on a Linux server, etc.
- Interview notes when discussing this requirement with assigned personnel

7.2.3 Required privileges are approved by authorized personnel.

- Documented access approval policies and procedures
- Interview notes when discussing this requirement with personnel covering approval of privileges

(continued)

7.2.4 All user accounts and related access privileges, including third-party/vendor accounts, are reviewed as follows:

- At least once every six months.
- To ensure user accounts and access remain appropriate based on job function.
- Any inappropriate access is addressed.
- Management acknowledges that access remains appropriate.

- Proof of user/third-party/vendor account reviews occurring at least once every six months.
- Proof any identified inappropriate access is addressed, for example, revoked, disabled etc.
- Proof that management has acknowledged the review(s) and access is still appropriate and implemented correctly.
- Change management system tickets and/or screenshots can provide proof.

7.2.5 All application and system accounts and related access privileges are assigned and managed as follows:

- Based on the least privileges necessary for the operability of the system or application.
- Access is limited to the systems, applications, or processes that specifically require their use.

- Documented access approval for application and system accounts
- Artifacts of least privileged access and assignment to applicable systems and applications, for example, configuration printout, screenshots, etc.

(continued)

7.2.5.1 All access by application and system accounts and related access privileges are reviewed as follows:

- Periodically (at the frequency defined in the entity's targeted risk analysis, which is performed according to all elements specified in Requirement 12.3.1).
- The application/system access remains appropriate for the function being performed.
- Any inappropriate access is addressed.
- Management acknowledges that access remains appropriate.

- Documented targeted risk analysis that outlines the frequency of review for all application and system accounts and related access privileges.
- Proof of application and system account reviews occurring at the rate outlined in the targeted risk analysis.
- Proof any identified inappropriate access is addressed, for example, revoked, disabled etc.
- Proof that management has acknowledged the review(s) and access is still appropriate and implemented correctly for all application and system accounts.
- Change management system tickets and/or screenshots can provide proof.

7.2.6 All user access to query repositories of stored cardholder data is restricted as follows:

- Via applications or other programmatic methods, with access and allowed actions based on user roles and least privileges.
- Only the responsible administrator(s) can directly access or query repositories of stored CHD.

- Documented policies and procedures defining user access to query repositories of stored payment card data
- Artifacts of configurations where this access to stored payment data is assigned and/or maintained, for example, screenshots, configuration settings, text document, etc.

(continued)

**7.3 Access to system components and data is managed via an access control
system(s).**

7.3.1 An access control system(s)
is in place that restricts access
based on a user's need to
know and covers all system
components.

- Artifacts from vendor documentation and
  system settings depicting all component
  access control systems, for example,
  operating system documentation,
  configuration documentation, etc.
- Proof that every in-scope component has an
  access control system that restricts access
  based on a user's need to know, for example,
  screenshot of an Active Directory listing with
  roles and assigned users combined with
  vendor documentation showing the system
  implementation is correct

7.3.2 The access control
system(s) is configured to
enforce permissions assigned
to individuals, applications,
and systems based on job
classification and function.

- Artifacts from vendor documentation and
  system settings depicting all component
  access control systems, for example,
  operating system documentation,
  configuration documentation, etc.
- Proof that every in-scope component has an
  access control system that restricts individual,
  application, and system access based on
  job classification and function, for example,
  vendor documentation showing the system
  implementation is correct

(continued)

7.3.3 The access control system(s) is set to "Deny All" by default.	• Artifacts from vendor documentation and system settings depicting all component access control systems, for example, operating system documentation, configuration documentation, etc. • Proof that every in-scope component has an access control system that is set to "Deny All" by default, for example, vendor documentation showing the system implementation is correct and the default "Deny All" rule is properly enforced

CHAPTER 9

Identify Users and Authenticate Access to System Components

Overview

Requirement 8 follows Requirement 7 in order and also in relation to keeping bad guys out of your payment environment. Requirement 7 mandates that we have a solid access control model and we have systems in place to perform access control on all components. Requirement 8 is basically the "Operations Manual" for the model and systems an entity has implemented to meet Requirement 7. In most of the requirements here, it is not very difficult to validate compliance, as there is not a lot of "gray" with Requirement 8. Nearly all of the test procedures are very "black and white."

The human element in any equation adds a certain amount of risk. People who are allowed to work on an entity's network, especially their

© Arthur B. Cooper Jr., Jeff Hall, David Mundhenk, Ben Rothke 2023
A. B. Cooper Jr. et al., *The Definitive Guide to PCI DSS Version 4*,
https://doi.org/10.1007/978-1-4842-9288-4_9

payment environment, may end up causing harm to the entity, perhaps by accident or intentionally. Downloading something that contains malware, opening a directory with sensitive information, and then sharing it with others are all daily occurrences on most company networks. People don't always intend to do things that cause harm, but it can happen just the same.

This is why it is so important for any entity that stores, processes, or transmits cardholder data to only provide access to an individual if that individual NEEDS such access to perform their job.

Fundamental Concepts

There are three fundamental concepts of identifying, authenticating, and authorizing users (or processes) with regard to an entity's cardholder data environment:

- *Establish identity*: This is very important. Why? Well, we need to know that someone or some process "IS" who they are representing themselves to "BE."

- *Authenticate identity*: Once identity has been established, it is then necessary for the person or process to prove their identity. This is the concept of authentication.

- *Authorization*: Once an identity is verified, what can the identity access? This is the concept of authorization.

Identity

In today's modern computing environments, individuals or processes are identified using some type of an identifier. Typically it will be a user, system, or application ID. The ID forms what is called an "account" that is used to establish identity and to ensure accountability can be assigned to the account as to all actions it "takes" or "makes" or "performs." This is why the use of shared or generic accounts is a big "no-no." If everyone is using the same account, how do we know who has done what? After a breach, can you imagine trying to prove who was to blame when everyone was using the account *goodguys*? This is why PCI is adamant about NO use of shared or generic accounts. In order to have full accountability, every ID or account must establish identity and then prove or verify the identity that was just established. The way this is done is through what we call authentication.

Authentication

In order to prove or verify identity, the concept of authentication must be fully understood. In order to AUTHENTICATE an identity, there are three "traditional" factors that are used:

- Something you know, such as a password or passphrase

- Something you have, such as a token device or smart card

- Something you are, such as a biometric element – fingerprint, retina scan, etc.

This has been the norm since the beginning of computing technologies and the authentication of the users of said technologies. At least one of these three factors must always be used. For added security, two-factor authentication (2FA) and multifactor authentication (MFA) are the concepts whereby two or more of the factors are used together in unison to prove the identity of the individual or process attempting to gain access. PCI bases all identity and authentication requirements on industry-accepted security principles. The US government produces an authoritative document known as *NIST Special Publication 800-63, Digital Identity Guidelines*. This document has a lot of information on identity and authentication.

Authorization

So, now that we have established the identity and authenticated the identity is "WHO" they claim to be, we have the concept of authorization. Authorization pertains to the "WHAT." Basically, what can this individual user, process, or system do now that they have been authenticated? For example, in a grocery store, cashiers probably have a very limited span of authorization on the systems they use to check out customers of the store. Typically, cashiers will only be able to start or stop the cash register or till, enter payment information, and accomplish the sale to the customer. Now, let's think about the manager of that same grocery store. This is an individual who may need access to many other capabilities on that cash register or till.

Perhaps the manager needs to be able to view all transactions for the day or shift, perform price changes, etc. These are all tasks the manager would be authorized to do based on their authenticated entity as "MANAGER," whereas the cashier would not be able to do these tasks based on their authenticated entity as "CASHIER."

All-Encompassing View

When assessing an organization's adherence to Requirement 8, one must take a holistic view of WHO has access to WHAT within the cardholder environment. The WHO could be a person or an application ID for an application that then allows personnel to view transactions in a database, or it could simply be a process running in a server that accomplishes an important task. As stated previously, Requirement 8 is basically like thinking about writing an "Operations Manual" for the model and systems an entity has implemented to meet Requirement 7. Fully understanding the access models defined in Requirement 7 makes it easy to understand Requirement 8, as it pertains to the actual "use" and "maintenance" of these access controls. Requirement 8 applies to the accounts on all system components, unless specifically called out in an individual sub-requirement, including but not limited to

- Point-of-sale accounts

- Accounts with administrative capabilities

- System and application accounts

- All accounts used to view or access cardholder data or to access systems with cardholder data

Requirements and Evidence

8.1 Processes and mechanisms for identifying users and authenticating access to system components are defined and understood.

8.1.1 All security policies and operational procedures that are identified in Requirement 8 are

- Documented
- Kept up to date
- In use
- Known to all affected parties

- Documented policies and procedures specified within section 8.x
- Interview notes

(*continued*)

8.1.2 Roles and responsibilities for performing activities in Requirement 8 are documented, assigned, and understood.	• Documented job roles and responsibilities covering all activities are properly assigned • Interview notes when discussing with individuals their authorized activities and understanding of them

8.2 User identification and related accounts for users and administrators are strictly managed throughout an account's lifecycle.

8.2.1 All users are assigned a unique ID before access to system components or cardholder data is allowed.	• Interview notes when discussing the fact ALL users are assigned unique account IDs • Documented proof that audit logs show all access to any component or especially cardholder data can be identified as to the individual account

(continued)

8.2.2 Group, shared, or generic accounts or other shared authentication credentials are only used when necessary on an exception basis and are managed as follows:

- Account use is prevented unless needed for an exceptional circumstance.
- Use is limited to the time needed for the exceptional circumstance.
- Business justification for use is documented.
- Use is explicitly approved by management.
- Individual user identity is confirmed before access to an account is granted.
- Every action taken is attributable to an individual user.

- Documented proof or screenshots for any use of shared/generic accounts. Ensure the artifact shows that these accounts are only used when necessary and on an exception basis and are managed in accordance with all elements specified in this requirement.
- Documented authentication policies and procedures to verify processes are defined for shared authentication credentials covering all of the elements in Requirement 8.
- Interview notes from discussions with administrators or responsible personnel when discussing the fact shared authentication credentials are only used when necessary and on an exception basis and are managed in accordance with all elements specified in this requirement.

(*continued*)

117

8.2.3 *Additional requirement for service providers only:* Service providers with remote access to customer premises use unique authentication factors for these customer premises.

Note   Any service provider being assessed that has access to customer/client systems, networks, premises, etc. must use unique authentication factors for remote access to these customer premises.

- Documented authentication policies and procedures covering all access to customer/client systems, networks, premises, etc.
- Interview notes from discussions with responsible personnel when discussing this type of access to customer/client systems, networks, premises, etc.

(continued)

8.2.4 Addition, deletion, and modification of user IDs, authentication factors, and other identifier objects are managed as follows:

- Authorized with the appropriate approval
- Implemented with only the privileges specified on the documented approval

- Documented authorizations across various phases of the account lifecycle (additions, modifications, and deletions)
- System artifacts, documents, screenshots, etc. showing system settings to show appropriate management of all authorizations is being accomplished
- Interview notes from discussions with responsible personnel when discussing this type of access to customer/ client systems, networks, premises, etc.

8.2.5 Access for terminated users is immediately revoked.

- Documented proof that terminated users are no longer on current user access lists. Typically screenshots from Active Directory, an LDAP server, etc. will show proof.
- Interview notes from discussions with responsible personnel when discussing all physical authentication factors – such as smart cards, tokens, etc. – have been returned or deactivated for terminated users.

(continued)

8.2.6 Inactive user accounts are removed or disabled within 90 days of inactivity.	• Documented proof that any inactive user accounts are removed or disabled within 90 days of inactivity. Typically screenshots from Active Directory, an LDAP server, etc. combined with audit log entries will show proof.
	• Interview notes from discussions with responsible personnel when discussing the fact that any inactive user accounts are removed or disabled within 90 days of inactivity.
8.2.7 Accounts used by third parties to access, support, or maintain system components via remote access are managed as follows: • Enabled only during the time period needed and disabled when not in use. • Use is monitored for unexpected activity.	• Documented proof that any accounts used by third parties for remote access are enabled only during the time period needed and disabled when not in use and all use is monitored for unexpected activity. This can be documentation of processes and procedures combined with screenshots and others.
	• Interview notes from discussions with responsible personnel when discussing third-party remote-access accounts.

(continued)

8.2.8 If a user session has been idle for more than 15 minutes, the user is required to reauthenticate to reactivate the terminal or session.

- System artifacts, documents, screenshots, etc. showing system settings where the system/session idle timeout features for user sessions have been set to 15 minutes or less.

8.3 Strong authentication for users and administrators is established and managed.

8.3.1 All user access to system components for users and administrators is authenticated via at least one of the following authentication factors:
- Something you know, such as a password or passphrase
- Something you have, such as a token device or smart card
- Something you are, such as a biometric element

- Documented proof that user access to system components is authenticated via at least one authentication factor
- Interview notes from discussions with responsible personnel when discussing each type of authentication factor used with each type of system component while observing an authentication for each "type" used to verify that authentication is functioning consistently with the documented authentication factor(s)

(continued)

8.3.2 Strong cryptography is used to render all authentication factors unreadable during transmission and storage on all system components.

- Vendor documentation for the systems and components used by the entity to show that authentication factors are rendered unreadable with strong cryptography during transmission and storage.
- System artifacts, documents, screenshots, etc. showing repositories of authentication factors to verify that they are unreadable during storage, for example, the Security Account Manager (SAM) database on a Windows Active Directory installation and others.
- With the assistance of the entity's technical staff, perform data transmission captures to verify that authentication factors are unreadable during transmission. This can be accomplished using TCPDUMP (on NIX systems) or perhaps using Wireshark or some other data capture software.

(continued)

8.3.3 User identity is verified before modifying any authentication factor.	• Documented procedures for modifying authentication factors that verify that when a user requests a modification of an authentication factor (e.g., password – something you know), the user's identity is verified before the authentication factor is modified • Interview notes from discussions with responsible personnel when discussing a user's identity is verified before the authentication factor is modified

(continued)

8.3.4 Invalid authentication attempts are limited by
- Locking out the user ID after not more than ten attempts
- Setting the lockout duration to a minimum of 30 minutes or until the user's identity is confirmed

- System artifacts, documents, screenshots, etc. showing that system settings and configurations are set to require that user accounts be locked out after not more than ten invalid logon attempts
- System artifacts, documents, screenshots, etc. showing that system settings and configurations are set to require that once a user account is locked out, it remains locked for a minimum of 30 minutes or until the user's identity is confirmed

8.3.5 If passwords/passphrases are used as authentication factors to meet Requirement 8.3.1, they are set and reset for each user as follows:
- Set to a unique value for first-time use and upon reset
- Forced to be changed immediately after the first use

- Documented procedures for setting and resetting passwords/passphrases (if used as authentication factors to meet Requirement 8.3.1)
- Interview notes from discussions with responsible personnel while observing to verify that passwords/ passphrases are set and reset in accordance with all elements specified in this requirement as documented in the entity's procedures

(continued)

8.3.6 If passwords/passphrases are used as authentication factors to meet Requirement 8.3.1, they meet the following minimum level of complexity: • A minimum length of 12 characters (or IF the system does not support 12 characters, a minimum length of eight characters) • Contains both numeric and alphabetic characters	• System artifacts, documents, screenshots, etc. showing that system settings and configurations are set to require that user password/passphrase complexity parameters are set in accordance with all elements specified in this requirement: 12 characters, numerics, and alphas. Typically screenshots from Active Directory, an LDAP server, etc. will show proof.
8.3.7 Individuals are not allowed to submit a new password/passphrase that is the same as any of the last four passwords/passphrases used.	• System artifacts, documents, screenshots, etc. showing that system settings and configurations are set to require that password parameters are set to require that new passwords/passphrases cannot be the same as the four previously used passwords/ passphrases. Typically screenshots from Active Directory, an LDAP server, etc. will show proof.

(continued)

8.3.8 Authentication policies and procedures are documented and communicated to all users including
- Guidance on selecting strong authentication factors
- Guidance for how users should protect their authentication factors
- Instructions not to reuse previously used passwords/passphrases
- Instructions to change passwords/passphrases if there is any suspicion or knowledge that the passwords/passphrases have been compromised and on how to report the incident

- Documented authentication policies and procedures including the elements specified in this requirement.
- Interview notes from discussions with responsible personnel and general users discussing the fact that policies and procedures are distributed to all users and users are familiar with authentication policies and procedures.
- Typically users are provided with these policies and procedures upon hire and are required to acknowledge and review them at least annually.

(continued)

8.3.9 If passwords/passphrases are used as the only authentication factor for user access (i.e., in any single-factor authentication implementation), then either • Passwords/passphrases are changed at least once every 90 days. OR • The security posture of accounts is dynamically analyzed, and real-time access to resources is automatically determined accordingly.	• System artifacts, documents, screenshots, etc. showing that system settings and configurations are set to require that passwords/passphrases are managed in accordance with ONE of the following: • Passwords/passphrases are changed at least once every 90 days. • The security posture of accounts is dynamically analyzed, and real-time access to resources is automatically determined accordingly.

(*continued*)

8.3.10 *Additional requirement for service providers only:* If passwords/passphrases are used as the only authentication factor for customer user access to cardholder data (i.e., in any single-factor authentication implementation), then guidance is provided to customer users including

- Guidance for customers to change their user passwords/passphrases periodically
- Guidance as to when, and under what circumstances, passwords/passphrases are to be changed

Note   For any service provider being assessed where passwords/passphrases are used as the only authentication factor for the service provider's customers with user access to cardholder data, then guidance must be provided to the service provider's customer users. When assessing a service provider like this, the assessor must gather the following evidence:

- Documented guidance provided to the service provider's customer users to verify that the guidance includes all elements specified in this requirement: changing passwords periodically and under what circumstances

(continued)

8.3.10.1 *Additional requirement for service providers only:* If passwords/passphrases are used as the only authentication factor for customer user access (i.e., in any single-factor authentication implementation), then either

- Passwords/passphrases are changed at least once every 90 days.

OR

- The security posture of accounts is dynamically analyzed, and real-time access to resources is automatically determined accordingly.

Note   For any service provider being assessed where passwords/passphrases are used as the only authentication factor for the service provider's customers with user access to cardholder data, then guidance must be provided to the service provider's customer users. When assessing a service provider like this, the assessor must gather the following evidence:

- System artifacts, documents, screenshots, etc. showing that system settings and configurations are set to require that service provider customer passwords/passphrases are managed in accordance with ONE of the following:
- Passwords/passphrases are changed at least once every 90 days.
- The security posture of accounts is dynamically analyzed, and real-time access to resources is automatically determined accordingly.

(*continued*)

8.3.11 Where authentication factors such as physical or logical security tokens, smart cards, or certificates are used

- Factors are assigned to an individual user and not shared among multiple users.
- Physical and/or logical controls ensure only the intended user can use that factor to gain access.

- Documented authentication policies and procedures to verify that procedures for using authentication factors such as physical security tokens, smart cards, and certificates are defined and include all elements specified in this requirement: tokens are not shared, and only the intended user may use the token to gain access.
- Interview notes from discussions with responsible personnel discussing the fact authentication factors are assigned to an individual user and not shared among multiple users.
- System artifacts, documents, screenshots, etc. to show that controls are implemented to ensure only the intended user can use that authentication token, factor, etc. to gain access.

(continued)

8.4 Multifactor authentication (MFA) is implemented to secure access into the CDE.

8.4.1 MFA is implemented for all non-console access into the CDE for personnel with administrative access.	• Network and/or system artifacts, documents, screenshots, etc. showing that network and/or system component settings and configurations are set to require that MFA is required for all non-console access into the CDE for any personnel with administrative access • Interview notes from discussions with responsible personnel when observing administrator personnel logging into the CDE and verifying that MFA is indeed required

(continued)

8.4.2 MFA is implemented for all access into the CDE.

Note   This requirement is considered a best practice until March 31, 2025, after which it will be required and must be fully considered during a PCI DSS assessment. It is nearly identical to Requirement 8.4.1 concerning administrative access into the CDE. The primary difference with this requirement is that ALL access into the CDE must use MFA as of March 31, 2025. Once this requirement has been implemented, the following evidence will need to be secured:

- Network and/or system artifacts, documents, screenshots, etc. showing that network and/or system component settings and configurations are set to require that MFA is required for all non-console access into the CDE.
- Interview notes from discussions with responsible personnel when observing any personnel (with access to the CDE) logging into the CDE and verifying that MFA is indeed required

(continued)

8.4.3 MFA is implemented for all remote network access originating from outside the entity's network that could access or impact the CDE as follows:

- All remote access by all personnel, both users and administrators, originating from outside the entity's network
- All remote access by third parties and vendors

- Network and/or system artifacts, documents, screenshots, etc. showing that network and/or system component settings on any remote servers or systems are set to require that MFA is required for all remote access by all personnel, both users and administrators, or third parties and vendors when said access originates from outside the entity's network
- Interview notes from discussions with responsible personnel when observing users and administrators connecting remotely to the network and verifying that multifactor authentication is required

(continued)

8.5 Multifactor authentication (MFA) systems are configured to prevent misuse.

8.5.1 MFA systems are implemented as follows:

- The MFA system is not susceptible to replay attacks.
- MFA systems cannot be bypassed by any users, including administrative users unless specifically documented and authorized by management on an exception basis, for a limited time period.
- At least two different types of authentication factors are used.
- Success of all authentication factors is required before access is granted.

- Vendor documentation for the systems and components used by the entity to show that the MFA system is not susceptible to replay attacks
- System artifacts, documents, screenshots, etc. showing that system configuration settings for the MFA implementation verify it is configured as such:
- The MFA system is not susceptible to replay attacks.
- The MFA systems cannot be bypassed by any users, including administrative users unless specifically documented and authorized by management on an exception basis, for a limited time period.
- At least two different types of authentication factors are used.
- Success of all authentication factors is required before access is granted.

(continued)

- Interview notes from observing processes to verify that any requests to bypass MFA are specifically documented and authorized by management on an exception basis, for a limited time period
- Interview notes from observing processes to verify personnel logging into system components in the CDE are granted access only after all authentication factors are successful
- Interview notes from observing personnel connecting remotely from outside the entity's network to verify that access is granted only after all authentication factors are successful

(*continued*)

8.6 Use of application and system accounts and associated authentication factors is strictly managed.

8.6.1 If accounts used by systems or applications can be used for interactive login, they are managed as follows:

- Interactive use is prevented unless needed for an exceptional circumstance.
- Interactive use is limited to the time needed for the exceptional circumstance.
- Business justification for interactive use is documented.
- Interactive use is explicitly approved by management.
- Individual user identity is confirmed before access to the account is granted.
- Every action taken is attributable to an individual user.

- Documented proof application and system accounts that can be used interactively are managed in accordance with all elements specified in this requirement
- Interview notes from discussions with responsible personnel to verify that application and system accounts are managed in accordance with all elements specified in this requirement

(*continued*)

8.6.2 Passwords/passphrases for any application and system accounts that can be used for interactive login are not hard-coded in scripts, configuration/property files, or bespoke and custom source code.

- Documented system development procedures proving that processes are defined for application and system accounts that can be used for interactive login, specifying that passwords/passphrases are not hard-coded in scripts, configuration/property files, or bespoke and custom source code
- Documented copies of scripts, configuration/property files, and bespoke and custom source code for application and system accounts that can be used for interactive login, to verify passwords/passphrases for those accounts are not present
- Interview notes from discussions with responsible development personnel to verify that processes are defined for application and system accounts that can be used for interactive login, specifying that passwords/passphrases are not hard-coded in scripts, configuration/property files, or bespoke and custom source code

(continued)

8.6.3 Passwords/passphrases for any application and system accounts are protected against misuse as follows:

- Passwords/passphrases are changed periodically (at the frequency defined in the entity's targeted risk analysis, which is performed according to all elements specified in Requirement 12.3.1) and upon suspicion or confirmation of compromise.
- Passwords/passphrases are constructed with sufficient complexity appropriate for how frequently the entity changes the passwords/passphrases.

- Documented policies and procedures proving that procedures are defined to protect passwords/passphrases for application or system accounts against misuse in accordance with all elements specified in this requirement
- Documented targeted risk analysis for the change frequency and complexity for passwords/passphrases used for interactive login to application and system accounts to verify the risk analysis was performed in accordance with all elements specified in Requirement 12.3.1 and addresses
- The frequency defined for periodic changes to application and system passwords/passphrases
- The complexity defined for passwords/passphrases and appropriateness of the complexity relative to the frequency of changes

(continued)

138

- System artifacts, documents, screenshots, etc. showing that system configuration settings verify that passwords/passphrases for any application and system accounts that can be used for interactive login are protected against misuse in accordance with all elements specified in this requirement
- Interview notes from discussions with responsible personnel to verify that passwords/passphrases for any application and system accounts that can be used for interactive login are protected against misuse in accordance with all elements specified in this requirement

CHAPTER 10

Restrict Physical Access to Cardholder Data

Overview

A key point to realize about information security is that nearly every operating system, from Windows to Linux and more, places the foundation of its security architecture at the physical server level. Unfortunately, physical security is more often an afterthought when deciding where to place a server. Such consequences can render payment servers and other devices with cardholder data (CHD) completely open to a security breach.

There are numerous things that are needed to create a foundation of comprehensive physical security for devices in the cardholder data environment (CDE). The foremost item to keep in mind is that all the security features in the world are valueless if the hardware and other media (USB drives, backup tapes, CD-ROM, etc.) are not physically secured. An organization must physically protect the devices themselves from any unauthorized access.

© Arthur B. Cooper Jr., Jeff Hall, David Mundhenk, Ben Rothke 2023
A. B. Cooper Jr. et al., *The Definitive Guide to PCI DSS Version 4*,
https://doi.org/10.1007/978-1-4842-9288-4_10

The security issue with physical access is that anyone who has physical access to a device can read file system data off that device. Even if a system is built with the highest levels of security assurance, it can't protect CHD if the operating system is not running. Someone can bypass the network operating system or simply tear out the hard drive and attempt to read the contents of the hard drive.

As an example, if someone has physical access to a server drive, they can use a low-level disk sector utility that can read the operating system partitions to read the data. The reason is that the files on a server are not stored in an encrypted format unless the administrator has specifically encrypted them.

There are many convincing reasons for needing physical security; a few of the most basic are preventing theft of equipment, preventing illegal access, preventing unauthorized use, and preventing intentional damage or destruction of the equipment.

The following three items should be part of a PCI physical security program:

Full control

Ensure that administrators have full control over the facility or server room.

Locks

Once you have a dedicated room, make sure you put a lock on the door. The ideal type of locking device is via a key card. This way, each entry can be tracked. Also, when someone loses authorization, they can easily and quickly be removed from the access group.

If key card access is not feasible, a combination door lock is acceptable. Both the combination door lock and key card provide the same level of security, but the key card makes authorization changes much easier to process. Whenever an authorized user is terminated, the combination must be changed immediately.

Authorization lists

Make a list of who is authorized to enter that room and place that list on the door. Ideally, that list should be as small as possible. System administrators and support personnel only should have access. Anyone whose name does not appear on the access list must be required to sign a visitor's log upon entering the room.

The function of the visitor's log is to see who is entering the room and which person is letting them in. It is important to note that visitor logs contain sensitive information that could be very useful to social engineers and thus must be treated as confidential information.

Visitor logs are essential for recording all third-party access to secure areas with CHD and require enough detail to provide for investigations should an event happen.

The implementation of this policy will ensure that the date and time that any third party was in the facility can be identified, along with the identity of the visitor.

A different school of thought states that a list of authorized personnel should not be placed on the entry door. The reason is that this would alert a devious individual that the room is somehow worth penetrating. This school of thought is that of security through obscurity. Security through obscurity might work for a short while but will eventually collapse. In the long run, such security will only detract from the overall security picture.

Obviously, you want the room to be as inconspicuous as possible, but not letting people know what is behind the doors may initiate curiosity and create more problems that could have originally been avoided. Don't advertise the server room, but don't try to deny its existence, either.

Pitfalls

Unless a facility has a mantrap (an access control device with a small space with two sets of interlocking doors, such that the first door must close before the second one opens), there will always be potential back doors into the CDE.

For example, tailgating is a concern. This is when an unauthorized person follows an authorized person into the CDE. While they can be expensive, anti-tailgating doors make tailgating almost impossible.

Social engineering is another significant physical security risk. A common example of that is someone holding a pizza or cup of coffee and walking into the secured area. An employee who happens to be there will hold the door open as they want to be courteous, but have let an unauthorized person into the CDE area.

Awareness about social engineering among your employees is an important thing to do. Having them be suspicious about any unusual activity or new people in the area can go a long way in obviating these physical security risks.

Point-of-Interaction Devices

The PCI SSC Glossary defines[1] a point of interaction as *the initial point where data is read from a card.* An electronic transaction acceptance product, a POI consists of hardware and software and is hosted in acceptance equipment to enable a cardholder to perform a card transaction. The POI may be attended or unattended. POI transactions are typically integrated circuit (chip) and/or magnetic stripe card-based payment transactions.

---

[1]`www.pcisecuritystandards.org/glossary/#glossary-p`

The POI specific requirements are found in Requirement 9.5 and are quite significant. Anyone whose infrastructure includes POI devices needs to ensure that the details of 9.5 are properly implemented.

As part of this, any PCI Point-to-Point Encryption (P2PE) devices are also included. The P2PE standard requires that CHD be encrypted upon use with the merchant's POS terminal. And it cannot be decrypted until processed by the payment processor. And the physical security controls are in scope, or all P2PE hardware.

Physical Security Applies Everywhere

Finally, when reviewing Requirement 9, it is easy to take a narrow view and think just about a data center. But physical security is not just for data centers. It is for every place where CHD can be stored, processed, or transmitted. And that often extends to call centers, remote offices, remote work locations in their homes, and much more.

There are countless locations that must be considered, and they will be in scope for Requirement 9. For a fast-food establishment, payment hardware is not just at the counter; there could be a payment gateway device in the manager's office or the break room. And all of these need to be secured.

Requirements and Evidence

9.1 Processes and mechanisms for restricting physical access to cardholder data are defined and understood.

9.1.1 All security policies and operational procedures that are identified in Requirement 9 are
- Documented
- Kept up to date
- In use
- Known to all affected parties

- Physical security policy
- Physical security processes

9.1.2 Roles and responsibilities for performing activities in Requirement 9 are documented, assigned, and understood.

- Roles and responsibilities matrix for those who support the CDE and/or have access to CHD, relevant to tasks for Requirement 9

9.2.1 Appropriate facility entry controls are in place to restrict physical access to systems in the CDE.

- QSA to perform a walk-through of the physical aspects of the CDE to ensure that the physical access controls in place are appropriate and meet the identified risks

(continued)

9.2 Physical access controls manage entry into facilities and systems containing cardholder data.

9.2.1.1 Individual physical access to sensitive areas within the CDE is monitored with either video cameras or physical access control mechanisms (or both) as follows:
- Entry and exit points to/from sensitive areas within the CDE are monitored.
- Monitoring devices or mechanisms are protected from tampering or disabling.
- Collected data is reviewed and correlated with other entries.
- Collected data is stored for at least three months, unless otherwise restricted by law.

- Inventory of cameras monitoring the CDE
- List of all physical security devices
- Evidence of how log data can't be modified
- Evidence of log storage for 90 days
- Random viewing of selected video clips of the CDE

9.2.2 Physical and/or logical controls are implemented to restrict use of publicly accessible network jacks within the facility.

- Evidence of how publicly accessible network jacks are disabled
- QSA to plug in a testing device to a sample of network jacks to ensure there is no connectivity

9.2.3 Physical access to wireless access points, gateways, networking/communications hardware, and telecommunication lines within the facility is restricted.

- Details of how wireless access points (WAPs) are secured from tampering
- QSA to view physical security controls and ensure they are adequate to address the risks

(continued)

| 9.2.4 Access to consoles in sensitive areas is restricted via locking when not in use. | • Evidence of how consoles are locked
• QSA to control a keyboard to a sample of consoles to ensure they are locked |

9.3 Physical access for personnel and visitors is authorized and managed.

| 9.3.1 Procedures are implemented for authorizing and managing physical access of personnel to the CDE, including
• Identifying personnel
• Managing changes to an individual's physical access requirements
• Revoking or terminating personnel identification
• Limiting access to the identification process or system to authorized personnel | • Physical security processes and procedures
• Details of how change access requests for physical devices are made
• Details of how access is granted to new employees and removed for terminated employees |

(continued)

9.3.1.1 Physical access to sensitive areas within the CDE for personnel is controlled as follows:

- Access is authorized and based on individual job functions.
- Access is revoked immediately upon termination.
- All physical access mechanisms, such as keys, access cards, etc., are returned or disabled upon termination.

9.3.2 Procedures are implemented for authorizing and managing visitor access to the CDE, including the following:

- Visitors are authorized before entering.
- Visitors are escorted at all times.
- Visitors are clearly identified and given a badge or another identification that expires.
- Visitor badges or another identification visibly distinguishes visitors from personnel.

- List of authorized users who have a justified need to be in a data center where there is CHD
- Process for returning any access token (SecurID fob, key card, etc.) when an employee with access to the CDE is terminated or voluntarily leaves the organization
- Process for removing access to networks, applications, systems, etc. for staff that is terminated or voluntarily leaves the organization

- Policy that defines the requirements for establishing physical access controls for visitors at all locations where CHD resides
- Process that details how visitors are handled, including visitor identification, escorting visitors, badging, repair people who show up without being called, data center and information systems department visitors, and the like

(continued)

9.3.3 Visitor badges or another identification is surrendered or deactivated before visitors leave the facility or at the date of expiration.

- Process for staff or visitors to wear an identification badge on their outer garments so that both the picture (if used) and information on the badge are clearly visible to all people with whom the wearer converses.
- Process for those who have forgotten their identification badge.
- Policy must include that employees or consultants must not permit unknown or unauthorized persons to pass through doors, gates, and other entrances to areas with CHD at the same time when authorized persons go through these entrances.

9.3.4 A visitor log is used to maintain a physical record of visitor activity within the facility and within sensitive areas, including

- The visitor's name and the organization represented
- The date and time of the visit
- The name of the personnel authorizing physical access
- Retaining the log for at least three months, unless otherwise restricted by law

- Ensure that there is a policy that requires a visitor log be maintained that contains the visitor's name, firm represented, and employee authorizing physical access to any data center or facility with CHD.
- Ensure there is a process for secure storage of visitor logs and that they are retained for at least three months.

(continued)

9.4 Media with cardholder data is securely stored, accessed, distributed, and destroyed.

9.4.1 All media with cardholder data is physically secured.	• Policy that defines security controls for all CHD stored, either in paper or electronic format
9.4.1.1 Offline media backups with cardholder data are stored in a secure location.	• Evidence showing the configuration of how offline backups with CHD are secured
	• Listings of any CHD stored in the cloud and evidence that the cloud service provider responsibility matrix has been reviewed and all client tasks are handled
9.4.1.2 The security of the offline media backup location(s) with cardholder data is reviewed at least once every 12 months.	• Evidence that the security of the offline media, including CHD stored in the cloud, is part of an annual risk assessment process and that it has been reviewed and approved
9.4.2 All media with cardholder data is classified in accordance with the sensitivity of the data.	• Evidence that any CHD stored is classified as per the corporate data classification policy

(*continued*)

9.4.3 Media with cardholder data sent outside the facility is secured as follows: • Media sent outside the facility is logged. • Media is sent by a secured courier or another delivery method that can be accurately tracked. • Offsite tracking logs include details about media location.	• Evidence that physical media containing CHD transferred out of the CDE is logged and that the transfer does not violate any PCI processing policies. • Review logs of all media transfers.
9.4.4 Management approves all media with cardholder data that is moved outside the facility (including when media is distributed to individuals).	• Evidence that physical media containing CHD transferred out of the CDE has management approval
9.4.5 Inventory logs of all electronic media with cardholder data are maintained.	• Review inventory of all media with CHD.
9.4.5.1 Inventories of electronic media with cardholder data are conducted at least once every 12 months.	• Evidence that a review of all media with CHD has been done within the past year • Evidence that there is a complete consolidation of all media

(continued)

9.4.6 Hard-copy materials with cardholder data are destroyed when no longer needed for business or legal reasons, as follows:
- Materials are cross-cut shredded, incinerated, or pulped so that cardholder data cannot be reconstructed.
- Materials are stored in secure storage containers prior to destruction.

- Process for the destruction of hard copies containing CHD
- If a third party is used for this requirement, evidence that the third party has been appropriately vetted and that the contract states that they will meet all PCI DSS requirements
- If a third party is used for this requirement, evidence that the third party is not merely recycling the hard copy

9.4.7 Electronic media with cardholder data is destroyed when no longer needed for business or legal reasons via one of the following:
- The electronic media is destroyed.
- The cardholder data is rendered unrecoverable so that it cannot be reconstructed.

- Review the information and media disposal policy to ensure that it defines controls for the proper disposal of all CHD, either in paper or electronic format.
- Review processes for data destruction, and ensure that proper sanitization processes are followed.
- Test a sample of media that has been overwritten or degaussed to ensure that all CHD has, in fact, been fully erased.

(continued)

9.5 Point-of-interaction (POI) devices are protected from tampering and unauthorized substitution.

9.5.1 POI devices that capture payment card data via direct physical interaction with the payment card form factor are protected from tampering and unauthorized substitution, including the following: • Maintaining a list of POI devices • Periodically inspecting POI devices to look for tampering or unauthorized substitution • Training personnel to be aware of suspicious behavior and to report tampering or unauthorized substitution of devices	• Review POI inventory. • Review the process for inspecting POI devices for tampering. • Review training material to ensure staff responsible for POI device security properly understand the necessary tasks.
9.5.1.1 An up-to-date list of POI devices is maintained, including • Make and model of the device • Location of the device • Device serial number or other methods of unique identification	• Review POI inventory. • Review a sample of devices and ensure that they are listed in the POI inventory.
9.5.1.2 POI device surfaces are periodically inspected to detect tampering and unauthorized substitution.	• Review the process for inspecting POI devices for tampering.

(continued)

154

9.5.1.2.1 The frequency of periodic POI device inspections and the type of inspections performed are defined in the entity's targeted risk analysis, which is performed according to all elements specified in Requirement 12.3.1.

- Review the risk assessment to ensure that the POI device inspection schedule is commensurate with the identified risk.
- Review logs to ensure that POI device inspections are done according to the defined schedule.

9.5.1.3 Training is provided for personnel in POI environments to be aware of attempted tampering or replacement of POI devices and includes

- Verifying the identity of any third-party persons claiming to be repair or maintenance personnel, before granting them access to modify or troubleshoot devices
- Procedures to ensure devices are not installed, replaced, or returned without verification
- Being aware of suspicious behavior around devices
- Reporting suspicious behavior and indications of device tampering or substitution to appropriate personnel

- Review training material to ensure it is adequate for those tasked to maintain the security of POI devices.
- Reviews POI device handling processes.
- Interview staff tasked with POI device security to ensure that they understand what their role is.

CHAPTER 11

Log and Monitor All Access to System Components and Cardholder Data

The overview for section 10.x of PCI DSS v4.0 reads as follows:

> *Logging mechanisms and the ability to track user activities are critical in preventing, detecting, or minimizing the impact of a data compromise. The presence of logs on all system components and in the cardholder data environment (CDE) allows thorough tracking, alerting, and analysis when something does go wrong. Determining the cause of a compromise is difficult, if not impossible, without system activity logs.*

Event logging, monitoring, auditing, and alerting are some of the most critically important processes in cybersecurity and are reflected similarly as well in the PCI DSS. Event logging also helps associate computer user activities with specific users and helps facilitate user accountability for their interactions with computing systems.

© Arthur B. Cooper Jr., Jeff Hall, David Mundhenk, Ben Rothke 2023
A. B. Cooper Jr. et al., *The Definitive Guide to PCI DSS Version 4*,
https://doi.org/10.1007/978-1-4842-9288-4_11

When systems are compromised by unauthorized user access, one of the first things an adversary will do is erase logs showing the compromise details and, later on, any logs that detail their unauthorized activities. That is why the PCI DSS also contains a requirement to export all critical event logs to a centralized internal server for archival preservation of the logs. Even if an adversary were able to erase localized system logs, their details are still preserved to aid with forensics analysis if needed. In addition, the section 10.x requirements for ensuring system clock synchronization via Network Time Protocol (NTP) help correlate adversarial activities across multiple sources in the event multiple systems are compromised. Lastly, event logging is also incredibly useful in helping troubleshoot events that occur up to and through system and application failures.

There are some new requirements in section 10.x of PCI DSS v4.0:

10.1.2: New requirement to document roles and responsibilities for all requirements in 10.x.

10.4.1: New requirement to support the use of automated tools for log reviews.

10.4.2.1: New requirement for a targeted risk analysis to define the frequency of periodic log reviews for all other system components not defined in Requirement 10.4.1.

10.5.1.1: New requirement for automated mechanisms for daily log reviews.

10.7.1.1: Includes the following for detecting, alerting, and reporting failures of critical security control systems:

- Automated log review mechanisms

- Automated code review tools

- Incident response software

10.7.1.2: Detect, alert, and report failures of critical security control systems.

Many of the above-mentioned requirements have been strongly recommended in the past by the PCI SSC and have been outright requirements for service providers. It is just another example of the PCI SSC constantly evaluating and enhancing PCI DSS requirements based upon enhanced evaluation of risk to CHD as well as feedback from the field.

Here are the 10.x requirements/sub-requirements and the artifacts required to validate compliance with them.

Requirements and Evidence

10.1 Processes and mechanisms for logging and monitoring all access to system components and cardholder data are defined and documented.

10.1.1 All security policies and operational procedures that are identified in Requirement 10 are • Documented • Kept up to date • In use • Known to all affected parties	• Documented logging security policies • Documented logging security procedures
10.1.2 Roles and responsibilities for performing activities in Requirement 10 are documented, assigned, and understood.	• Documented roles and responsibilities policy

---

(*continued*)

10.2 Audit logs are implemented to support the detection of anomalies and suspicious activity and the forensic analysis of events.

10.2.1 Audit logs are enabled and active for all system components and cardholder data.	• Screenshot samples showing logging is enabled for all components
10.2.1.1 Audit logs capture all individual user access to cardholder data.	• Screenshot samples showing logging is enabled for all access to cardholder data (such as encrypted CHD in a database table)
10.2.1.2 Audit logs capture all actions taken by any individual with administrative access, including any interactive use of application or system accounts.	• Sample audit logs showing administrator access is being logged
10.2.1.3 Audit logs capture all access to audit logs.	• Screenshot samples showing individual access to audit logs is also being logged
10.2.1.4 Audit logs capture all invalid logical access attempts.	• Sample audit logs showing invalid access attempts are being logged
10.2.1.5 Audit logs capture all changes to identification and authentication credentials including but not limited to • Creation of new accounts • Elevation of privileges • All changes, additions, or deletions to accounts with administrative access	• Sample audit logs showing capture of all changes to identification and authentication credentials

(*continued*)

10.2.1.6 Audit logs capture the following:
- All initialization of new audit logs
- All starting, stopping, or pausing of the existing audit logs

- Sample audit logs showing capture of all initialization, starting, stopping, or pausing

10.2.1.7 Audit logs capture all creation and deletion of system-level objects.

- Sample audit logs showing capture of all creation and deletion of system-level objects

10.2.2 Audit logs record the following details for each auditable event:
- User identification
- Type of event
- Date and time
- Success and failure indication
- Origination of event
- Identity or name of affected data, system component, resource, or service (e.g., name and protocol)

- Sample audit logs showing capture of the following for each auditable event:
  - User identification
  - Type of event
  - Date and time
  - Success and failure indication
  - Origination of event
  - Identity or name of affected data, system component, resource, or service

10.3 Audit logs are protected from destruction and unauthorized modifications.

10.3.1 Read access to audit log files is limited to those with a job-related need.

- Screenshot of RBACs for log access

10.3.2 Audit log files are protected to prevent modifications by individuals.

- Screenshot of RBACs that shows they are "read-only"

(continued)

10.3.3 Audit log files, including those for external-facing technologies, are promptly backed up to a secure, central, internal log server(s) or another media that is difficult to modify.	• Screenshot of centralized logging resources • Sample audit logs
10.3.4 File integrity monitoring or change detection mechanisms are used on audit logs to ensure that existing log data cannot be changed without generating alerts.	• Screenshot of FIM configurations • Screenshot of configuration that shows that existing log data cannot be changed without generating alerts

10.4 Audit logs are reviewed to identify anomalies or suspicious activity.

10.4.1 The following audit logs are reviewed at least once daily: • All security events • Logs of all system components that store, process, or transmit CHD and/or SAD • Logs of all critical system components • Logs of all servers and system components that perform security functions (e.g., network security controls, intrusion detection systems/ intrusion prevention systems (IDS/IPS), authentication servers)	• Documentation that shows that logs are being reviewed on a daily basis in accordance with the aforementioned requirements
10.4.1.1 Automated mechanisms are used to perform audit log reviews.	• Screenshots of the automated mechanisms used to perform audit log reviews

(continued)

10.4.2 Logs of all other system components (those not specified in Requirement 10.4.1) are reviewed periodically.	• Documentation that shows that other types of logs are being reviewed on a periodic basis in accordance with the aforementioned requirements
10.4.2.1 The frequency of periodic log reviews for all other system components (not defined in Requirement 10.4.1) is defined in the entity's targeted risk analysis, which is performed according to all elements specified in Requirement 12.3.1.	• This new requirement for a targeted risk analysis carries a high risk for non-compliance. Firms must ensure this is adequately addressed. • Targeted risk analysis report that specifies the frequency of periodic log reviews.
10.4.3 Exceptions and anomalies identified during the review process are addressed.	• Documentation that shows exceptions and anomalies identified during the review process are addressed

10.5 Audit log history is retained and available for analysis.

10.5.1 Retain audit log history for at least 12 months, with at least the most recent three months immediately available for analysis.	• Documentation showing that audit log history is kept for at least 12 months and that three months of logs are immediately available

(continued)

10.6 Time synchronization mechanisms support consistent time settings across all systems.

10.6.1 System clocks and time are synchronized using time synchronization technology.

- Screenshots that show system clocks and time are synchronized using time synchronization technology

10.6.2 Systems are configured to the correct and consistent time as follows:

- One or more designated time servers are in use.
- Only the designated central time server(s) receives time from external sources.
- Time received from external sources is based on International Atomic Time or Coordinated Universal Time (UTC).
- The designated time server(s) accepts time updates only from specific industry-accepted external sources.
- Where there is more than one designated time server, the time servers peer with one another to keep accurate time.
- Internal systems receive time information only from the designated central time server(s).

- Documentation that demonstrates that this requirement and all sub-requirements are being met (screenshots are acceptable)

(continued)

10.6.3 Time synchronization settings and data are protected as follows:
- Access to time data is restricted to only personnel with a business need.
- Any changes to time settings on critical systems are logged, monitored, and reviewed.

- RBACs showing access controls for access to time data
- Documentation that demonstrates any changes to time settings on critical systems are logged, monitored, and reviewed

10.7 Failures of critical security control systems are detected, reported, and responded to promptly.

10.7.1 *Additional requirement for service providers only.* Failures of critical security control systems are detected, alerted, and addressed promptly, including but not limited to failure of the following critical security control systems:
- Network security controls
- IDS/IPS
- FIM
- Anti-malware solutions
- Physical access controls
- Logical access controls
- Audit logging mechanisms
- Segmentation controls (if used)

- IR policy that demonstrates failures of critical security control systems are detected, alerted, and addressed promptly
- Incident response reports showing this requirement and sub-requirements are being met

(continued)

10.7.2 Failures of critical security control systems are detected, alerted, and addressed promptly, including but not limited to failure of the following critical security control systems:

- Network security controls
- IDS/IPS
- Change detection mechanisms
- Anti-malware solutions
- Physical access controls
- Logical access controls
- Audit logging mechanisms
- Segmentation controls (if used)
- Audit log review mechanisms
- Automated security testing tools (if used)

- Documentation that demonstrates that failures of critical security control systems are detected, alerted, and addressed promptly

(continued)

10.7.3 Failures of any critical security control systems are responded to promptly, including but not limited to

- Restoring security functions
- Identifying and documenting the duration (date and time from start to end) of the security failure
- Identifying and documenting the cause(s) of failure and documenting required remediation
- Identifying and addressing any security issues that arose during the failure
- Determining whether further actions are required as a result of the security failure
- Implementing controls to prevent the cause of failure from reoccurring
- Resuming monitoring of security controls

- IR reports and change control documents that demonstrate that failures of any critical security control systems are responded to promptly for all sub-requirements

CHAPTER 12

Test Security of Systems and Networks Regularly

Overview/Intro

IT environments of today are, by definition and their overall complexities, highly dynamic in nature. One of the few confirmable and consistent attributes of such environments is that they are in a constant state of change, always in a perpetual state of updates, configuration changes, adds/moves, commissioning/decommissioning, and patching. Cloud environments can be even more dynamic than on-premise networks due to their capability to support the scale-up and scale-down of IT resources and services based upon demand. In fact, some cloud environments are actually torn down and rebuilt every 24 hours. Cardholder data environments (CDEs) are no different.

© Arthur B. Cooper Jr., Jeff Hall, David Mundhenk, Ben Rothke 2023
A. B. Cooper Jr. et al., *The Definitive Guide to PCI DSS Version 4*,
https://doi.org/10.1007/978-1-4842-9288-4_12

Such technological sprawl and constant state of flux elevate the need for the regular testing of security controls of systems and networks. The PCI DSS has a long history of mandating that CDEs be regularly tested for the existence of vulnerabilities and the need to update security patches. PCI DSS v4.0 continues that tradition but "raises the bar" with respect to some new requirements. Here are the new requirements for 11.x:

11.1.2: New requirement to document all roles and responsibilities for all applicable requirements for such in 11.x.

11.3.1.1: New requirement to manage all other applicable vulnerabilities (those not ranked as high risk or critical) found during internal vulnerability scans. *This requirement is a best practice until March 31, 2025.* (Note: A measurable percentage of breaches still continue to be attributable to exploitable flaws in applications. In addition, low- and medium-risk vulnerabilities in applications can be leveraged in tandem or in some sequential order such that they can cumulatively add up to higher-risk vulnerability profiles. It is strongly recommended that merchants and service providers implement this new requirement well before March 31, 2025.)

11.3.1.2: New requirement for assessed entities to perform internal vulnerability scans via authenticated scanning. *This requirement is a best practice until March 31, 2025.*

11.4.7: New requirement for multi-tenant service providers to support their customers for external penetration testing. *This requirement is a best practice until March 31, 2025.*

11.5.1.: New requirement for service providers to use intrusion detection and/or intrusion prevention techniques to detect, alert on/ prevent, and address covert malware communication channels. *This requirement is a best practice until March 31, 2025.*

11.6.1: New requirement to deploy a change-and-tamper detection mechanism to alert for unauthorized modifications to the HTTP headers and contents of payment pages as received by the consumer browser. *This requirement is a best practice until March 31, 2025.*

The last requirement mentioned is a really big deal and should be considered in conjunction with PCI DSS 6.3.4 regarding script injection in client-side web browsers. Generally speaking, the client-side web browser attack surface has been completely overlooked as a threat landscape except by malware authors, the hacking community, social media, and mass marketers. All of these threat actors and business intelligence collectors continue to manipulate, and even exploit, end user client-side browser vulnerabilities for ill-gotten gain and often under the guise of gathering "critical user business intelligence."

In addition, traditional penetration testing and application security assessment tools, methods, and techniques tend to neglect this attack surface. They focus primarily on server-side vulnerabilities, not the client-side web browser. As such, Personally Identifiable Information (PII) including payment card data and user authentication credentials is routinely harvested with relative impunity by threat actors. This has been the case for some time now. Thankfully, the PCI SSC has finally defined requirements for reducing and/or eliminating the risk to payment card pages and payment card redirection pages with respect to this issue.

Requirements and Evidence

11.1 Processes and mechanisms for regularly testing security of systems and networks are defined and understood.

11.1.1 All security policies and operational procedures that are identified in Requirement 11 are • Documented • Kept up to date • In use • Known to all affected parties	• Documented security policies and operational procedures mandated by 11.x

---

(continued)

11.1.2 Roles and responsibilities for performing activities in Requirement 11 are documented, assigned, and understood.	• Documented roles and responsibilities mandated by 11.x

11.2 Wireless access points are identified and monitored, and unauthorized wireless access points are addressed.

11.2.1 Authorized and unauthorized wireless access points are managed as follows: • The presence of wireless (Wi-Fi) access points is tested. • All authorized and unauthorized wireless access points are detected and identified. • Testing, detection, and identification occur at least once every three months. • If automated monitoring is used, personnel are notified via generated alerts.	• Documented policies and procedures for WAP monitoring and testing for rogue WAPs • Documented rogue WAP test results
11.2.2 An inventory of authorized wireless access points is maintained, including a documented business justification.	• Documented inventory and business justification of all authorized WAPs

(continued)

11.3 External and internal vulnerabilities are regularly identified, prioritized, and addressed.

11.3.1 Internal vulnerability scans are performed as follows:

- At least once every three months.
- High-risk and critical vulnerabilities (per the entity's vulnerability risk rankings defined in Requirement 6.3.1) are resolved.
- Rescans are performed that confirm all high-risk and critical vulnerabilities (as noted previously) have been resolved.
- The scan tool is kept up to date with latest vulnerability information.
- Scans are performed by qualified personnel, and organizational independence of the tester exists.

- Documented vulnerability scanning policy and procedures
- Vulnerability scanning reports that show no high-risk or critical vulnerabilities
- Change control tickets showing high and critical risk issue remediation
- Rescan reports showing high-risk and critical vulnerabilities have been remediated
- Screenshot of the scanning tool software version

11.3.1.1 All other applicable vulnerabilities (those not ranked as high risk or critical per the entity's vulnerability risk rankings defined in Requirement 6.3.1) are managed as follows:

- Addressed based on the risk defined in the entity's targeted risk analysis, which is performed according to all elements specified in Requirement 12.3.1.
- Rescans are conducted as needed.

- Documented risk analysis showing applicable vulnerabilities not ranked as high risk or critical per the entity's vulnerability risk rankings as evaluated
- Sample rescan reports to show that rescans are conducted as needed

(continued)

11.3.1.2 Internal vulnerability scans are performed via authenticated scanning as follows: • Systems that are unable to accept credentials for authenticated scanning are documented. • Sufficient privileges are used for those systems that accept credentials for scanning. • If accounts used for authenticated scanning can be used for interactive login, they are managed in accordance with Requirement 8.2.2.	• Documented vulnerability scanning policy and procedures • Documentation that shows "authenticated" vulnerability scans are taking place
11.3.1.3 Internal vulnerability scans are performed after any significant change as follows: • High-risk and critical vulnerabilities (per the entity's vulnerability risk rankings defined in Requirement 6.3.1) are resolved. • Rescans are conducted as needed. • Scans are performed by qualified personnel, and organizational independence of the tester exists (not required to be a QSA or ASV).	• Documented vulnerability scanning policy • Vulnerability scanning reports that show no high-risk or critical vulnerabilities • Change control tickets showing high-risk and critical remediation

(continued)

11.3.2 External vulnerability scans are performed as follows: • At least once every three months. • By a PCI SSC Approved Scanning Vendor (ASV). • Vulnerabilities are resolved, and ASV Program Guide requirements for a passing scan are met. • Rescans are performed as needed to confirm that vulnerabilities are resolved per the ASV Program Guide requirements for a passing scan.	• Documented vulnerability scanning policy • Vulnerability scanning reports that show no high-risk or critical vulnerabilities • Change control tickets showing high-risk and critical remediation • Rescan reports showing high-risk and critical vulnerabilities have been remediated • Screenshot of the scanning tool software version
11.3.2.1 External vulnerability scans are performed after any significant change as follows: • Vulnerabilities that are scored 4.0 or higher by the CVSS are resolved. • Rescans are conducted as needed. • Scans are performed by qualified personnel, and organizational independence of the tester exists (not required to be a QSA or ASV).	• Documented vulnerability scanning policy and procedures • Vulnerability scanning reports that show no vulnerabilities with a CVSS score of 4.0 or higher • Change control tickets showing CVSS 4.0+ scores are remedied • Rescan reports showing high-risk and critical vulnerabilities have been remediated

(continued)

11.4 External and internal penetration testing is regularly performed, and exploitable vulnerabilities and security weaknesses are corrected.

11.4.1 A penetration testing methodology is defined, documented, and implemented by the entity and includes:

- Industry-accepted penetration testing approaches
- Coverage for the entire CDE perimeter and critical systems
- Testing from both inside and outside the network
- Testing to validate any segmentation and scope reduction controls
- Application-layer penetration testing to identify, at a minimum, the vulnerabilities listed in Requirement 6.2.4
- Network-layer penetration tests that encompass all components that support network functions as well as operating systems
- Review and consideration of threats and vulnerabilities experienced in the last 12 months
- Documented approach to assessing and addressing the risk posed by exploitable vulnerabilities and security weaknesses found during penetration testing
- Retention of penetration testing results and remediation activity results for at least 12 months

- Documented penetration testing policy and procedures that address all the bulleted controls detailed within this requirement

(continued)

176

11.4.2 Internal penetration testing is performed: • Per the entity's defined methodology. • At least once every 12 months. • After any significant infrastructure or application upgrade or change. • By a qualified internal resource or qualified external third party. • Organizational independence of the tester exists (not required to be a QSA or ASV).	• Penetration testing policy and procedures • Sample penetration testing report(s) • Validation of penetration tester qualifications to do the work • Proof of penetration tester organizational independence
11.4.3 External penetration testing is performed: • Per the entity's defined methodology. • At least once every 12 months. • After any significant infrastructure or application upgrade or change. • By a qualified internal resource or qualified external third party. • Organizational independence of the tester exists (not required to be a QSA or ASV).	• Penetration testing policy and procedures • Sample penetration testing report(s) • Validation of penetration tester qualifications to do the work • Proof of penetration tester organizational independence
11.4.4 Exploitable vulnerabilities and security weaknesses found during penetration testing are corrected as follows: • In accordance with the entity's assessment of the risk posed by the security issue as defined in Requirement 6.3.1. • Penetration testing is repeated to verify the corrections.	• Sample reports that show that exploitable vulnerabilities are remediated (before and after reports demonstrating issue resolution)

(continued)

11.4.5 If segmentation is used to isolate the CDE from other networks, penetration tests are performed on segmentation controls as follows:

- At least once every 12 months and after any changes to segmentation controls/methods.
- Covering all segmentation controls/methods in use.
- According to the entity's defined penetration testing methodology.
- Confirming that the segmentation controls/methods are operational and effective and isolate the CDE from all out-of-scope systems.
- Confirming effectiveness of any use of isolation to separate systems with differing security levels (see Requirement 2.2.3).
- Performed by a qualified internal resource or qualified external third party.
- Organizational independence of the tester exists (not required to be a QSA or ASV).

- Penetration testing policy and procedures that demonstrate segmentation testing is compliant
- Sample penetration testing report(s)
- Proof of penetration tester organizational independence

(continued)

11.4.6 *Additional requirement for service providers only.* If segmentation is used to isolate the CDE from other networks, penetration tests are performed on segmentation controls as follows:
- At least once every six months and after any changes to segmentation controls/methods.
- Covering all segmentation controls/methods in use.
- According to the entity's defined penetration testing methodology.
- Confirming that the segmentation controls/ methods are operational and effective and isolate the CDE from all out-of-scope systems.
- Confirming effectiveness of any use of isolation to separate systems with differing security levels (see Requirement 2.2.3).
- Performed by a qualified internal resource or qualified external third party.
- Organizational independence of the tester exists (not required to be a QSA or ASV).

- Penetration testing policy and procedures demonstrating compliance with all the bulleted sub-requirements described in 11.4.6
- Sample penetration testing reports

11.4.7 *Additional requirement for multi-tenant service providers only.* Multi-tenant service providers support their customers for external penetration testing per Requirements 11.4.3 and 11.4.4.

- Penetration testing policy and procedures demonstrating compliance with all the bulleted sub-requirements described in 11.4.7
- Sample penetration testing reports

(continued)

11.5 Network intrusions and unexpected file changes are detected and responded to.

11.5.1 Intrusion detection and/or intrusion prevention techniques are used to detect and/or prevent intrusions into the network as follows:
- All traffic is monitored at the perimeter of the CDE.
- All traffic is monitored at critical points in the CDE.
- Personnel are alerted to suspected compromises.
- All intrusion detection and prevention engines, baselines, and signatures are kept up to date.

- Logical network drawing(s) demonstrating the deployment location(s)
- Screenshots of the IDS/IPS management console showing agent configurations and alerting capability
- Screenshot of the IDS/IPS versioning and signature status

11.5.1.1 *Additional requirement for service providers only*. Intrusion detection and/or intrusion prevention techniques detect, alert on/prevent, and address covert malware communication channels.

- Screenshots of the IDS/IPS configuration capability to detect, alert on/prevent, and address covert malware communication channels

11.5.2 A change detection mechanism (e.g., file integrity monitoring tools) is deployed as follows:
- To alert personnel to unauthorized modification (including changes, additions, and deletions) of critical files
- To perform critical file comparisons at least once weekly

- Documented change detection policy
- List of all change control attributes tracked and alerted upon
- Sample critical file comparison reports

(continued)

11.6 Unauthorized changes on payment pages are detected and responded to.

11.6.1 A change and tamper detection mechanism is deployed as follows:

- To alert personnel to unauthorized modification (including indicators of compromise, changes, additions, and deletions) to the HTTP headers and the contents of payment pages as received by the consumer browser.
- The mechanism is configured to evaluate the received HTTP header and payment page.
- The mechanism functions are performed as follows:

– At least once every seven days

OR

– Periodically (at the frequency defined in the entity's targeted risk analysis, which is performed according to all elements specified in Requirement 12.3.1)

- Client-side web browser change and tamper detection policy
- Screenshot(s) of change detection configuration(s)
- Sample test reports demonstrating its effectiveness to support all the sub-requirements in 11.6.1

CHAPTER 13

Support Information Security with Organizational Policies and Programs

Overview

While PCI is centered around protecting cardholder data (CHD), Requirement 12 is central to all data. Requirement 12 is about data and IT governance, which is relevant to any organization.

Everything in Requirement 12 falls into the category of basic information security controls. This includes fundamentals such as risk management, security policies, awareness and end user training, and more.

© Arthur B. Cooper Jr., Jeff Hall, David Mundhenk, Ben Rothke 2023
A. B. Cooper Jr. et al., *The Definitive Guide to PCI DSS Version 4*,
https://doi.org/10.1007/978-1-4842-9288-4_13

The Need for Information Security Policies

Companies need information system security policies for the same
reason all regulations, in general, are needed: to ensure a safe and sound
infrastructure. For companies that want to stop employees, policies are
the first step in ensuring that corporate assets are not squandered by some
nefarious employees.

By way of analogy, why is it that when a powerful earthquake hits
California, scores of people die, in addition to collateral structural
damage? But when an earthquake with the same magnitude hits a third-
world country, why is it that tens of thousands of people die in addition to
entire towns being reduced to rubble? The answer is obvious; California
has a well-developed, organized, and enforced set of building rules and
regulations. These rules and regulations take the risk of earthquakes
into consideration, and all buildings are required to be built to deal with
that risk.

Those countries that don't require the same set of stringent building
rules and regulations may save on initial construction costs, but when
disaster strikes, the effects are atrocious and horrific. Unfortunately, the
state of computer security and corresponding policies and procedures in
most US organizations are much closer to that of third-world countries.

Risk Management

Another of the key areas in Requirement 12 is risk management.
W. Edwards Deming astutely observed that "if you can't measure it, you
can't manage it." When it comes to securing CHD, there is no single way to
secure it. The appropriate ways to do that are dependent on the underlying
risk. A billion-dollar ecommerce vendor won't use the same approach to
PCI security as a 50-person medical practice.

And with that, the only way a firm can know which level of security to implement is if they first perform a risk assessment to understand what their unique and specific risks are. An information security risk assessment mandated as per Requirement 12.3 identifies and assesses the risks to networks, applications, the CDE, staff, and more. Carrying out a risk assessment allows an organization to deal with the risks holistically, rather than relying on generic industry best practices.

Sy Syms, the founder of the clothing company that bore his name, had an advertising tagline of "an educated consumer is our best customer." From a PCI perspective, a company that understands its risk is a PCI DSS best customer. Due to the fact that since they understand what their risks are, they will be better able to ensure no breach of CHD.

Countless books have been written on how to perform a risk assessment. At a high level, most of them all center around the following four basic aspects:

1. *Risk identification*: Determine where the CHD resides and any other CDE assets. For each asset, or asset type, create risk profiles.

2. *Assessment*: Identify the security risks for all assets from step 1. Then, determine what resources are needed to mitigate the identified risks.

3. *Mitigation*: Define your risk mitigation approach and what the security controls for each risk will be.

4. *Prevention*: Use the necessary security tools to minimize the risks from entering the CDE.

What's New in Version 4.0

With DSS version 4, the Council added an updated core requirement heading to reflect the focus on corporate policies and programs that support information security around PCI.

One thing to consider is that PCI is indeed a point-in-time assessment. The PCI Security Standards Council (PCI SSC) wants merchants and service providers to consider a PCI compliance as a continuous process. A number of new requirements were added to emphasize this.

There were a lot of changes to Requirement 12. Version 4 brings 11 new requirements to Requirement 12. A full listing is in the official document Summary of Changes from PCI DSS Version 3.2.1 to 4.0,[1] which you should definitely review.

Some of the other significant changes to Requirement 12 include

- *12.3.1*: This requirement is mentioned 22 times in the DSS, so you know it needs to be taken seriously. With 12.3.1, you have the flexibility to determine how frequently to perform certain compliance efforts, based on your targeted risk analysis. Take the time to do this right, as many of the requirements that reference 12.3.1 are significantly dependent on it. If you do 12.3.1 wrong or don't document your approach, it can have a significant negative trickle-down effect to your ability to achieve PCI compliance.

---

[1] https://docs-prv.pcisecuritystandards.org/PCI%20DSS/Standard/
PCI-DSS-v3-2-1-to-v4-0-Summary-of-Changes-r2.pdf?agreement=true&t
ime=1649151196749

- *12.5.2*: New requirement for entities to document
  and confirm their PCI DSS scope annually and upon
  significant change to their in-scope environment. In the
  past, many entities would scope their PCI environment
  once and assume it was static. This new requirement
  ensures that entities stay on top of the PCI scope.

- *12.5.2.1*: New requirement for service providers to
  document and confirm their PCI DSS scope at least
  once every six months and upon significant change to
  the in-scope environment.

- *12.10.4.1*: New requirement to perform a targeted risk
  analysis to define the frequency of periodic training for
  incident response personnel.

- *12.10.7*: New requirement for incident response
  procedures to be in place and initiated upon
  detection of a stored PAN anywhere where it is not
  expected to be.

Requirements and Evidence

12.1 A comprehensive information security policy that governs and provides direction for protection of the entity's information assets is known and current.

12.1.1 An overall information security policy is

- Established
- Published
- Maintained
- Disseminated to all relevant personnel, as well as to relevant vendors and business partners

- Copies of all relevant information security policies
- Evidence of policies that support all of the 12 PCI requirements

12.1.2 The information security policy is
- Reviewed at least once every 12 months
- Updated as needed to reflect changes to business objectives or risks to the environment

- Evidence of how the annual information security policy process is done
- Evidence of management review and sign-off of all relevant information security policies

12.1.3 The security policy clearly defines information security roles and responsibilities for all personnel, and all personnel are aware of and acknowledge their information security responsibilities.

- Ensure that the information security policies have a responsibility assignment matrix that details the participation of various roles in completing PCI and security tasks.
- Ideally, there should be a RACI table where relevant tasks are: responsible, accountable, consulted, and informed.

(continued)

12.1.4 Responsibility for information security is formally assigned to a chief information security officer or another information security knowledgeable member of executive management.

- In line with Requirement 12.1.3, evidence that senior management ensures that information security tasks have been delegated to team members that have the qualifications to perform those tasks

12.2 Acceptable use policies for end user technologies are defined and implemented.

12.2.1 Acceptable use policies for end user technologies are documented and implemented, including
- Explicit approval by authorized parties
- Acceptable uses of the technology
- List of products approved by the company for employee use, including hardware and software

- Show acceptable use policies that cover all aspects of IT. These include requirements for the secure use and management of electronic mail, minimum requirements and responsibilities for the secure connection and use of the Internet and other public networks by employees and contractors when accessing in-scope systems, employee and third-party access to the CDE, and overall acceptable use of all company computer and communication system assets.

(continued)

12.3 Risks to the cardholder data environment are formally identified, evaluated, and managed.

12.3.1 Each PCI DSS requirement that provides flexibility for how frequently it is performed (e.g., requirements to be performed periodically) is supported by a targeted risk analysis that is documented and includes:

- Identification of the assets being protected
- Identification of the threat(s) that the requirement is protecting against
- Identification of factors that contribute to the likelihood and/or impact of a threat being realized
- Resulting analysis that determines, and includes justification for, how frequently the requirement must be performed to minimize the likelihood of the threat being realized
- Review of each targeted risk analysis at least once every 12 months to determine whether the results are still valid or if an updated risk analysis is needed
- Performance of updated risk analyses when needed, as determined by the annual review

- Evidence that the risk management requirements for the identification of the appropriate control posture for all 12 PCI DSS requirements have been carried out.
- Show how the firm has undertaken a risk assessment of all threats, vulnerabilities, and exposures that could impact CHD and services. This risk assessment needs to be done at least annually and upon significant changes to the environment.

(*continued*)

12.3.2 A targeted risk analysis is performed for each PCI DSS requirement that the entity meets with the customized approach, to include

- Documented evidence detailing each element specified in "Appendix D: Customized Approach" (including, at a minimum, a controls matrix and risk analysis)
- Approval of documented evidence by senior management
- Performance of the targeted analysis of risk at least once every 12 months

- Evidence that the risk management requirements for the identification of the appropriate control posture for all 12 PCI DSS requirements have been carried out.
- Show how the firm has undertaken a risk assessment of all threats, vulnerabilities, and exposures that could impact CHD and services. This risk assessment needs to be done at least annually and upon significant changes to the environment.

12.3.3 Cryptographic cipher suites and protocols in use are documented and reviewed at least once every 12 months, including at least the following:

- An up-to-date inventory of all cryptographic cipher suites and protocols in use, including purpose and where used

- Detailed inventory of cryptographic cipher suites in use.
- Ensure that the policy contains details around cryptographic controls, the use of cryptographic controls, and key management.

(continued)

- Active monitoring of industry trends regarding continued viability of all cryptographic cipher suites and protocols in use
- A documented strategy to respond to anticipated changes in cryptographic vulnerabilities

- When developing a cryptographic policy, the following shall be considered:
  - The management approach toward the use of cryptographic controls across the organization, including the general principles under which business information should be protected.
  - Based on a risk assessment, the required level of protection shall be identified taking into account the type, strength, and quality of the encryption algorithm required.
  - The use of encryption for the protection of information transported by mobile or removable media devices or across communication lines.
  - The approach to key management, including methods to deal with the protection of cryptographic keys and the recovery of encrypted information in the case of lost, compromised, or damaged keys.

(continued)

12.3.4 Hardware and software technologies in use are reviewed at least once every 12 months, including at least the following:

- Analysis that the technologies continue to receive security fixes from vendors promptly
- Analysis that the technologies continue to support (and do not preclude) the entity's PCI DSS compliance
- Documentation of any industry announcements or trends related to a technology, such as when a vendor has announced "end-of-life" plans for a technology
- Documentation of a plan, approved by senior management, to remediate outdated technologies, including those for which vendors have announced "end-of-life" plans

- This is a new requirement that carries a high risk for non-compliance if not properly addressed.
- List of end-of-life forecasts for all hardware and software technologies in use.
- Based on the inventory of in-scope system components, ensure that these system components are reviewed for PCI compliance. For all of these components, ensure that they are fully patched.
- For in-scope system components managed by a third party, review their PCI Attestation of Compliance (AOC) and validate that it is current.
- For in-scope system components that are not compliant, create a compensating control or determine when the end of life for the components will be.

(*continued*)

12.4 PCI DSS compliance is managed.

12.4.1 *Additional requirement for service providers only.* Responsibility is established by executive management for the protection of cardholder data and a PCI DSS compliance program to include

- Overall accountability for maintaining PCI DSS compliance
- Defining a charter for a PCI DSS compliance program and communication to executive management

- Review the service providers' PCI charter. Ensure that it has assigned the overall responsibility to maintain PCI DSS compliance to executive management, for accountability.

12.4.2 *Additional requirement for service providers only.* Reviews are performed at least once every three months to confirm that personnel are performing their tasks in accordance with all security policies and operational procedures. Reviews are performed by personnel other than those responsible for performing the given task and include, but are not limited to, the following tasks:

- Daily log reviews
- Configuration reviews for network security controls
- Applying configuration standards to new systems
- Responding to security alerts
- Change management processes

- Show evidence that these quarterly reviews were done over the last 12 months.

(continued)

194

12.4.2.1 *Additional requirement for service providers only:* Reviews conducted in accordance with Requirement 12.4.2 are documented to include

- Results of the reviews
- Documented remediation actions taken for any tasks that were found to not be performed in Requirement 12.4.2
- Review and sign-off of results by personnel assigned responsibility for the PCI DSS compliance program

- Show evidence that these quarterly reviews were done over the last 12 months.

12.5 PCI DSS scope is documented and validated.

12.5.1 An inventory of system components that are in scope for PCI DSS, including a description of function/use, is maintained and kept current.

- Complete listing of every component in the CDE.
- Ensure that there are adequate details of its specific function.
- As per the sampling guidelines, sample a few components to ensure that the inventory is accurate and up to date.

(continued)

12.5.2 PCI DSS scope is documented and confirmed by the entity at least once every 12 months and upon significant change to the in-scope environment. At a minimum, the scoping validation includes

- Identifying all data flows for the various payment stages (e.g., authorization, capture settlement, chargebacks, and refunds) and acceptance channels (e.g., card-present, card-not-present, and ecommerce)
- Updating all data flow diagrams per Requirement 1.2.4
- Identifying all locations where account data is stored, processed, and transmitted, including but not limited to (1) any locations outside of the currently defined CDE, (2) applications that process CHD, (3) transmissions between systems and networks, and (4) file backups
- Identifying all system components in the CDE, connected to the CDE, or that could impact security of the CDE
- Identifying all segmentation controls in use and the environment(s) from which the CDE is segmented, including justification for environments being out of scope

- Show evidence of how the PCI was defined.
- Show data flow documentation that follows the CHD and that it matches the master scope documentation.

(continued)

- Identifying all connections from third-party entities with access to the CDE
- Confirming that all identified data flows, account data, system components, segmentation controls, and connections from third parties with access to the CDE are included in scope

12.5.2.1 *Additional requirement for service providers only.* PCI DSS scope is documented and confirmed by the entity at least once every six months and upon significant change to the in-scope environment. At a minimum, the scoping validation includes all the elements specified in Requirement 12.5.2

- Show evidence of how the PCI was defined.
- Show data flow documentation that follows the CHD and that it matches the master scope documentation.
- Provide management sign-off on how this is reviewed every six months.

12.5.3 *Additional requirement for service providers only.* Significant changes to organizational structure result in a documented (internal) review of the impact to PCI DSS scope and applicability of controls, with results communicated to executive management.

- If a significant change has been made to the CDE, provide evidence that it has been reviewed by management and that no additional risks have been introduced via the change.

(continued)

197

12.6 Security awareness education is an ongoing activity.

12.6.1 A formal security awareness program is implemented to make all personnel aware of the entity's information security policy and procedures and their role in protecting the cardholder data.

- Review PCI security awareness program training materials.
- Review security awareness program policy and process.

12.6.2 The security awareness program is

- Reviewed at least once every 12 months
- Updated as needed to address any new threats and vulnerabilities that may impact the security of the entity's CDE or the information provided to personnel about their role in protecting cardholder data

- Review PCI security awareness program training materials to ensure they are current and address topics relevant to the organization.

12.6.3 Personnel receive security awareness training as follows:

- Upon hire and at least once every 12 months.
- Multiple methods of communication are used.
- Personnel acknowledge at least once every 12 months that they have read and understood the information security policy and procedures.

- Review evidence that every employee has taken security awareness training within the last year.
- Review the awareness materials to ensure that they meet PCI DSS requirements and that the awareness topics are relevant and germane.

(continued)

198

12.6.3.1 Security awareness training includes awareness of threats and vulnerabilities that could impact the security of the CDE, including but not limited to • Phishing and related attacks • Social engineering	• Review the awareness materials to ensure that they meet these PCI DSS requirements.
12.6.3.2 Security awareness training includes awareness about the acceptable use of end user technologies in accordance with Requirement 12.2.1.	• Review the awareness materials to ensure that they meet these PCI DSS requirements for those employees that are using the specific technologies within the CDE.

12.7 Personnel are screened to reduce risks from insider threats.

12.7.1 Potential personnel who will have access to the CDE are screened, within the constraints of local laws, prior to hire to minimize the risk of attacks from internal sources.	• Ensure that the human resources policy mandates that external applicants selected to fill any position within the organization will be required to pass a background investigation prior to the first day of employment.

12.8 Risk to information assets associated with third-party service provider (TPSP) relationships is managed.

12.8.1 A list of all third-party service providers (TPSPs) with which account data is shared or that could affect the security of account data is maintained, including a description for each of the services provided.	• Review the list of all third-party service providers (TPSPs) that have connectivity or access to the CHD.

(*continued*)

12.8.2 Written agreements with TPSPs
are maintained as follows:

- Written agreements are maintained
  with all TPSPs with which account
  data is shared or that could affect the
  security of the CDE.
- Written agreements include
  acknowledgments from TPSPs that
  they are responsible for the security
  of account data the TPSPs possess or
  otherwise store, process, or transmit
  on behalf of the entity or to the extent
  that they could impact the security of
  the entity's CDE.

- Review contracts of these TPSPs to
  ensure that they contractually agree to
  meet PCI requirements.

12.8.3 An established process is
implemented for engaging TPSPs,
including proper due diligence prior to
engagement.

- Review the third-party security
  management policy to ensure it
  defines the requirements for the
  management of third-party services
  that handle CHD.

12.8.4 A program is implemented to
monitor TPSPs' PCI DSS compliance
status at least once every 12 months.

- Review evidence that all TPSPs are PCI
  compliant.
- Show evidence that the AOC of all of
  the in-scope TPSPs has been obtained,
  reviewed, and verified to be PCI
  compliant.

(continued)

12.8.5 Information is maintained about which PCI DSS requirements are managed by each TPSP, which are managed by the entity, and any that are shared between the TPSP and the entity.	• Review the TPSPs' PCI DSS responsibility matrix. • Ensure that it is an appropriately detailed matrix of PCI DSS requirements, including the description of whether responsibility for each individual control lies with the TPSP or their customer or whether responsibility is shared between both parties.

12.9 Third-party service providers (TPSPs) support their customers' PCI DSS compliance.

12.9.1 *Additional requirement for service providers only*: TPSPs acknowledge in writing to customers that they are responsible for the security of account data they possess or otherwise store, process, or transmit on behalf of the customers or to the extent that they could impact the security of the customers' CDE.	• Ensure that it is an appropriately detailed matrix of PCI DSS requirements, including the description of whether responsibility for each individual control lies with the TPSP or their customer or whether responsibility is shared between both parties, and that this is signed off.

(continued)

12.9.2 *Additional requirement for service providers only:* TPSPs support their customers' requests for information to meet Requirements 12.8.4 and 12.8.5 by providing the following upon customer request:

- PCI DSS compliance status information for any service the TPSP performs on behalf of customers (Requirement 12.8.4)
- Information about which PCI DSS requirements are the responsibility of the TPSP and which are the responsibility of the customer, including any shared responsibilities (Requirement 12.8.5)

- Review documentation and associated contracts that all TPSPs have agreed to meet this requirement.

(continued)

**12.10 Suspected and confirmed security incidents that could impact the CDE
are responded to immediately.**

12.10.1 An incident response plan (IRP)
exists and is ready to be activated in
the event of a suspected or confirmed
security incident. The plan includes but is
not limited to

- Roles, responsibilities, and
  communication and contact strategies
  in the event of a suspected or
  confirmed security incident, including
  notification of payment brands and
  acquirers, at a minimum
- Incident response procedures with
  specific containment and mitigation
  activities for different types of
  incidents
- Business recovery and continuity
  procedures
- Data backup processes
- Analysis of legal requirements for
  reporting compromises
- Coverage and responses of all critical
  system components
- Reference or inclusion of incident
  response procedures from the
  payment brands

- Review the incident response policy,
  incident response plan (IRP), and
  associated processes to ensure they
  meet and address all relevant PCI DSS
  requirements.
- Ensure that the IRP notes that all
  suspected CHD breaches will be
  reported to and investigated by
  appropriately trained individuals within
  the company. And when a breach is
  confirmed, action will be taken to lock
  down systems and escalate it to the
  appropriate bodies.

(continued)

12.10.2 At least once every 12 months, the security incident response plan is
- Reviewed and the content is updated as needed
- Tested, including all elements listed in Requirement 12.10.1

- Review the incident response plan and ensure that it has been updated to reflect current PCI compliance levels.

12.10.3 Specific personnel are designated to be available on a 24/7 basis to respond to suspected or confirmed security incidents.

- Review the incident response call tree to ensure staff is available and aware of their duties and responsibilities 24/7.

12.10.4 Personnel responsible for responding to suspected and confirmed security incidents are appropriately and periodically trained on their incident response responsibilities.

- PCI QSA should speak with a sample of members of the incident response team to verify that they understand their responsibilities for PCI DSS incident response.
- Review any relevant training records of the incident response team to ensure their capabilities and that they are adequately trained.

12.10.4.1 The frequency of periodic training for incident response personnel is defined in the entity's targeted risk analysis, which is performed according to all elements specified in Requirement 12.3.1.

- Review risk documentation to determine the defined training intervals.
- Correlate the defined training intervals to the training records.

(continued)

12.10.5 The security incident response plan includes monitoring of and responding to alerts from security monitoring systems, including but not limited to

- Intrusion detection and intrusion prevention systems.
- Network security controls.
- Change detection mechanisms for critical files.
- The change and tamper detection mechanism for payment pages. This bullet is a best practice until its effective date; refer to the following Applicability Notes for details.
- Detection of unauthorized wireless access points.

- Review the security incident response plan to ensure it meets all of the PCI DSS requirements.

12.10.6 The security incident response plan is modified and evolved according to lessons learned and to incorporate industry developments

- Review any post-mortem reports from previous incidents and ensure the lessons learned from those incidents have been incorporated into the current security incident response plan.

(continued)

12.10.7 Incident response procedures
are in place, to be initiated upon the
detection of a stored PAN anywhere it is
not expected, and include

- Determining what to do if a PAN is
  discovered outside the CDE, including
  its retrieval, secure deletion, and/or
  migration into the currently defined
  CDE, as applicable
- Identifying whether sensitive
  authentication data is stored with
  a PAN
- Determining where the account data
  came from and how it ended up
  where it was not expected
- Remediating data leaks or process
  gaps that resulted in the account data
  being where it was not expected

- Review incident response policy
  and procedures to ensure PAN data
  breaches are defined.
- Speak with members of the incident
  response team to ensure they
  understand how to identify PAN data
  and processes to understand how it
  can be determined if there is a breach.

CHAPTER 14

How to Read a Service Provider Attestation of Compliance

Reading a service provider Attestation of Compliance (AOC) is a necessary skill that is not taught or not taught entirely. Anyone that has been through a PCI assessment is familiar with the AOC document. The PCI AOC declares an organization's compliance with PCI DSS. The AOC serves as documented evidence that the organization has the cardholder security practices in place to effectively protect against threats to its cardholder data (CHD).

For an AOC to be effective, it must be signed off by a PCI Qualified Security Assessor (QSA) or by the merchant of record for the business.

However, there are some special items in the AOC for service providers that organizations that rely on these service providers need to know about, as well as how to interpret them. It is up to every organization to perform these reviews as their own PCI compliance depends on it.

The first is in "Part 2a. Scope Verification" for services that were included. This section lists all the services that were included in the assessment you are relying upon. If any service your organization is relying upon is not listed here, then it was not included in the assessment, and you cannot use this AOC to rely upon for anything related to that service.

© Arthur B. Cooper Jr., Jeff Hall, David Mundhenk, Ben Rothke 2023
A. B. Cooper Jr. et al., *The Definitive Guide to PCI DSS Version 4*,
https://doi.org/10.1007/978-1-4842-9288-4_14

Part 2a also has a section for services that were not included in the assessment. If your service was not in the included area, then check to see if it is listed here. If it is not listed here, then it is likely that it either has not been assessed or was overlooked when the service list was created. Either way, you will need to contact the service provider and find out where you can obtain an AOC for any missing services.

The second important section is "Part 2d. In-Scope Locations/ Facilities." This section needs to be reviewed to ensure that your services' facilities are listed here. You cannot rely on the AOC if they are not listed. As with the included/not included service lists, you will need to contact the service provider to determine what AOC you need to obtain if your location is not listed.

A key point here is that you have a choice if you determine that your services or locations are not listed. You can demand that the service provider provide you with an AOC for those services and locations, or you can include the services and locations as part of your assessment. Each has issues related to timing when getting an AOC and including it in your assessment and cost if you include the work in your assessment.

The third key section is "Part 2g. Summary of Assessment." This is where the service provider documents the 12 requirements and two appendices of what was tested and the testing results. With v4, this section now lists all the possible responses (i.e., In Place, Not Applicable, Not Tested, and Not In Place) and if a compensating control or customized approach was used.

What is typically missing from this section is a detailed list of those requirements within the gross requirement that were Not In Place, Not Tested, Not Applicable, etc. That more complete controls matrix will now have to be provided as a separate document from the service provider. You will need a controls matrix from the service provider to comply with Requirement 12.8.5 in your PCI assessment. Many service providers have provided a more complete controls matrix for several years as part of their AOC package to customers.

The fourth section is Part 3, which will tell you the assessment date, on which you will need to complete your third-party management table in your own assessment. The date is also important to ensure that you are using the latest AOC for a service provider and to prove that you are truly monitoring your vendors.

Nothing is more embarrassing than giving a QSA an old AOC and then explaining that you really do monitor your service providers. Worse is claiming that the service provider is responsible for a requirement and the QSA explaining after reviewing the controls matrix that the service provider has stated otherwise.

The final important area is Part 4, which lists the Action Plan for Non-compliant Requirements. With the advent of v4, this section only is to be completed if there were areas identified that were judged non-compliant.

As the Council pointed out at the 2022 Community Meeting, this was technically true with prior versions of the DSS, but most QSAs and others filled it out because we had been trained that all boxes needed to be checked or filled out. Regardless, if something is documented as not in place, your organization must monitor the situation with the service provider until it is resolved.

Another point to make about service providers with non-compliance conditions is that the PCI DSS does not say that non-compliant service providers cannot be used. However, the card brands do have rules regarding the use of non-compliant service providers, so you may be out of compliance with a given card brand's rules if a service provider is non-compliant.

Getting the AOC from the Service Provider Should Be Easy

A final observation: Just because an AOC is supplied does not necessarily mean you should trust it. Myriad details buried in the AOC can attest to how adequate the service provider's level of security truly is.

A good indicator of a service provider's level of compliance is the ease with which they share their AOC. They should be more than happy to share it with any party with a legitimate interest in seeing it.

As written in "A tale of two PCI AOCs,"[1] how you receive the AOC from the service provider can often determine the actual level of their PCI compliance.

Most service providers have their AOC on their website, and it should take no more than a few minutes to download it.

Also, you want to make sure your service provider has completed the correct AOC. Service providers can only use the Service Provider SAQ D or the Report on Compliance. The authors have seen many instances where the service provider did not complete the proper PCI form. It is also not unusual to receive a Merchant AOC from a service provider that accepts payment cards for their services when asking for their service provider AOC.

And when you have a QSA signing the AOC, ensure that both the individual QSA and the QSA firm are listed[2] on the PCI website as being currently certified. Some organizations have their CEO or similar C-level individual to sign their AOCs. In most cases, these individuals are not QSAs but are still allowed to sign the AOC because they are the legal officials of the organization.

Many service providers state in marketing material and on Facebook, LinkedIn, and the like that they are PCI compliant. But if you really want to know how compliant they are, the ease with which they make their AOC available is often a good indicator.

---

[1] https://medium.com/p/77712a40b242

[2] https://listings.pcisecuritystandards.org/assessors_and_solutions/ qualified_security_assessors

CHAPTER 15

Segmentation and Tokenization

Segmentation is one of the most misunderstood aspects of PCI compliance. Many people read too deeply into the DSS about segmentation. On page 12 of PCI DSS version 4,[1] it states that *segmentation of the CDE from the remainder of an entity's network is not a PCI DSS requirement*. The next sentence, though, does clarify that segmentation is strongly recommended as a method that may reduce the:

- Scope of the PCI DSS assessment

- Cost of the PCI DSS assessment

- Cost and difficulty of implementing and maintaining PCI DSS controls

- Risk to an organization relative to payment card account data (reduced by consolidating that data into fewer, more controlled locations)

---

[1] https://docs-prv.pcisecuritystandards.org/PCI%20DSS/Standard/PCI-DSS-v4_0.pdf

© Arthur B. Cooper Jr., Jeff Hall, David Mundhenk, Ben Rothke 2023
A. B. Cooper Jr. et al., *The Definitive Guide to PCI DSS Version 4*,
https://doi.org/10.1007/978-1-4842-9288-4_15

Without adequate segmentation, the entire network is in scope for the PCI DSS assessment. Segmentation can be achieved using a number of physical or logical methods, such as properly configured internal network security controls, routers with strong access control lists, or other technologies that restrict access to a particular segment of a network.

To be considered out of scope for PCI DSS, a system component must be properly segmented (isolated) from the CDE, such that the out-of-scope system component could not impact the security of the CDE, even if that component was compromised.

David and Ben wrote "Lightening the PCI Load: Solutions to Reduce PCI Scope"[2] way back in 2009. PCI compliance scoping was then, and still is, an intensively debated topic, even among PCI Qualified Security Assessors (QSAs).

The spirit and intent of that article and their follow-up piece "End-to-End Encryption: The PCI Security Holy Grail"[3] provided some clarity and an approach to help organizations reduce PCI DSS compliance scope to the absolute minimum.

Even the PCI Guru has weighed in with a series of blog posts over the years on network segmentation. The last of these was in 2020 with the PCI Council's release of their "Information Supplement on Scoping and Segmentation."[4]

The bottom line in all of these discussions is that network segmentation is a key to reducing PCI scope as we will discuss later on in this chapter.

---

[2] www.csoonline.com/article/2123913/lightening-the-pci-load--solutions-to-reduce-pci-scope.html

[3] www.csoonline.com/article/2124346/end-to-end-encryption--the-pci-security-holy-grail.html

[4] https://pciguru.wordpress.com/2020/04/30/the-last-hopefully-scoping-discussion/

Much has changed since then: the ubiquitous adoption of virtualized systems and tokenization; the introduction of streamlined and stripped-down ecommerce solutions, including those that are shared hosted; the implementation of encrypt-at-the-swipe payment card solutions; EMV-compatible processing; and more.

As technology, processes, and people have marched forward, the promise of measurable PCI scope reduction appears to have been offset by questions and concerns concerning the scoping of new technology implementations. Just as was the case when PCI DSS version 1 was released, many are still struggling to come to grips with PCI compliance scoping, even with PCI DSS version 4.

Why Segment?

Network segmentation has long been used to increase performance and simplify management. From a PCI perspective, it's not an actual PCI DSS requirement, but should be considered a best practice to help prevent successful attacks.

PCI DSS states that any device involved in the storage, processing, or transmission of cardholder data (CHD) is considered part of the segment. To keep things as simple as possible, designers should segment the network to include only those resources that are needed for transaction processing and storage. Segmentation can help reduce costs associated with your PCI assessment and just plain offers better security – when it comes to the CDE, more restricted access is better.

PCI Guidance on Segmentation

For years, merchants have complained of a lack of guidance around segmentation from the PCI Security Standards Council (SSC). The SSC heard the complaints, recognized this, and, in December 2016, published official guidance and clarification in "Information Supplement: Guidance for PCI DSS Scoping and Network Segmentation."[5] One of the most critical efforts in this regard came to fruition and is manifested by a clarification around what constitutes a PCI in-scope system.

To review, PCI applies to all system components included in or connected to the cardholder data environment (CDE). The CDE comprises people, processes, and technologies that store, process, or transmit CHD or sensitive authentication data.

The official definition[6] of a system component is any network component, server, or application included in or connected to the CDE. Some examples of system components include but are not limited to

- Systems that provide security services (authentication servers), facilitate segmentation (internal firewalls), or may impact the security of (name resolution or web redirection servers) the CDE

- Virtualization components (virtual machines, virtual switches/routers, virtual appliances, virtual applications/desktops, hypervisors)

- Network components (firewalls, switches, routers, wireless access points, network appliances, other security appliances)

- Servers (web, application, database, authentication, mail, proxy, timing, DNS)

---

[5]www.pcisecuritystandards.org/documents/Guidance-PCI-DSS-Scoping-and-Segmentation_v1.pdf

[6]www.pcisecuritystandards.org/pci_security/glossary#S

- Applications (purchased and custom, internally and externally developed)

- Any other component or device located within or connected to the CDE

Added to these components is the follow-up section on what constitutes adequate logical segmentation, and it would appear that the PCI SSC has finally clarified these topics to a level that makes PCI compliance scoping a straightforward endeavor. Much progress has been made to help merchants and service providers get this right. However, there continues to be much confusion and consternation as to the implications of such new clarifications in the face of new PCI technologies and processes.

Segmentation Is Not a Trivial Task

For those that find themselves with a payment infrastructure that is not adequately segmented, the redesign and rearchitecture needed to properly segment is a significant task. The time needed to redesign and deploy systems, including necessary testing, is something that can take many months.

Defining Your CDE

As any QSA can tell you, clients will often be at their most creative element when they try to define what their cardholder data environment (CDE) scope is and isn't. This is because the smaller the scope, the less work they and the QSA have to do. Clients will often do contortions in describing their networks, to have much of it deemed out of scope. While creativity is a good thing, their attempts to explain away how their networks transmitting cardholder data (CHD) and thousands of devices storing CHD are somehow out of PCI scope can often border on the delusional.

Perhaps the best definition of PCI scope comes from Coop, who says that determining what your CDE is comes down to this, as Coop astutely noted: "Follow the cardholder data. Wherever it goes, that is your initial scope. Then figure out what connects to all of that, and you have your final scope."

In those 27 words, Coop stops all the contortions, denials, inventions, and more of what constitutes a CDE. If you don't want your CDE to include thousands of devices, hundreds of endpoints, and all of your data center equipment, you should not have let it grow to that in the first place.

Tokenization and PCI

Full details about tokenization can be found in "Information Supplement: PCI DSS Tokenization Guidelines."[7] Although this document is 11 years old, the core information is the same.

Tokenization is a process by which the primary account number (PAN) is replaced with a surrogate value called the *token*. De-tokenization is the reverse process of redeeming a token for its associated PAN value. The security of an individual token relies predominantly on the infeasibility of determining the original PAN knowing only the surrogate value.

Depending on the particular implementation of a tokenization solution, tokens used within merchant systems and applications may not need the same level of security protection associated with the use of PANs. Storing tokens instead of PANs is one alternative that can help reduce the

---

[7] www.pcisecuritystandards.org/documents/Tokenization_Guidelines_Info_ Supplement.pdf

amount of CHD in the CDE, potentially reducing the merchant's effort to implement PCI DSS requirements.

Simply put, one of the best ways to reduce PCI scope is via tokenization. It is the consensus of all four authors of this book that for most organizations, there is absolutely no need to store CHD. Unless there is an absolutely compelling reason to store CHD (and there are very, very few), tokenization is something that you should have in place now or be seriously considering.

And by not storing CHD, an entity can reduce almost all of their PCI compliance requirements. That is a proverbial win/win.

CHAPTER 16

The Customized Approach, Compensating Controls, and the Targeted Risk Analysis

Overview

PCI has always allowed folks to use "compensating controls" to meet any requirement they are unable to meet using the defined control within the PCI requirements. This has been the norm for all versions of the PCI DSS until now. Version 4.0 brings us the new "customized approach." Ever since the 2019 PCI North America Community Meeting in Vancouver when many of us heard the PCI SSC present the idea of a customized

© Arthur B. Cooper Jr., Jeff Hall, David Mundhenk, Ben Rothke 2023
A. B. Cooper Jr. et al., *The Definitive Guide to PCI DSS Version 4*,
https://doi.org/10.1007/978-1-4842-9288-4_16

approach to PCI requirements, we sort of scratched our heads; or at least
we scratched them until we figured out what the "customized approach"
really meant.

The other chapters in this book covering each requirement are focused
on using the standard, defined approach to validate PCI compliance.
Rather than attempt to split each requirement into two different validation
methods, it was decided to look at the new customized approach by itself
and explain the why, what, and how of it all.

This chapter covers the process of using the "customized approach" in
a generic sense. This was by design, as any attempt at defining all possible
customizations for all requirements would not be practical.

Two Implementation and
Validation Approaches

In order to fully understand how customized controls can be implemented
and now have an official sanctioned validation approach, we need to
discuss each validation approach and be able to understand them both:

- *Defined approach*: This is the validation methodology
  we have outlined throughout this book for each
  requirement. It is the only way one has been able to
  validate their compliance with PCI requirements since
  the requirements were originally released for use. It can
  still be used, and in most cases it makes much more
  sense for an entity to still use this approach. Using this
  approach should be well-known to anyone who has
  any experience at all with PCI. Using this approach
  mandates the assessed entity design and implement

security controls that will meet the requirements as they are written. The assessor (Internal Security Assessor (ISA) or Qualified Security Assessor (QSA)) is then responsible to follow the written testing procedures and verify the requirements have all been met.

- *Customized approach*: This new sanctioned approach focuses on the overall objective of the requirement rather than the requirements and testing procedures as written. If it seems confusing, it can be if you allow it to be. Try to envision a situation where the assessed entity implements controls to meet the "customized" approach objective. WOW! That's interesting, right? When using this approach, every implementation will be different as there are "NO" defined testing procedures, and the assessor will actually be responsible to come up with testing procedures that "WILL" adequately test the entity's customized implementation. It's very important that the assessor can validate the entity's customized, implemented controls "MEET" the stated "customized approach objective" contained in the requirements.

Compensating Controls vs. the Customized Approach

Now that you have some idea of what the customized approach is, let's discuss the differences between using a compensating control (which has been done since the beginning of PCI) and using the customized approach. Compensating controls are generally used in situations where

221

there is a legacy system, software, or process that cannot be updated to meet the requirement as written. It's always been a fact that compensating controls could be used if one or both of the following were true:

1. Entity has a DOCUMENTED technical constraint.

2. Entity has a DOCUMENTED business constraint.

Most assessors will tell you that the "technical" problem an entity has is that they need to buy some new equipment, servers, hardware, software, etc., but they can't afford it – which then becomes a "business" problem. Generally, using compensating controls means an entity can't afford to fix the technical problem, so they claim they have a DOCUMENTED business constraint. Not always, but generally this rings true 98% of the time. There is even a new requirement (12.3.4) to keep track of end-of-life plans for hardware and applications.

Compensating controls have been used improperly for many years, and it's great to see that v4.0 of the PCI DSS includes a clarification in Appendix B that compensating controls cannot be used to retroactively address a requirement that was "missed" in the past or just didn't get "done." This has never been the intent of using a compensating control. Unfortunately, many times entities used compensating controls when something that should have been done wasn't done and nothing was done to address it. Shame on all the assessors out there, ISAs or QSAs, who allowed this to happen.

Compensating controls are still an option within the defined approach for entities with a legitimate, DOCUMENTED technical or business constraint that prevents them from meeting the defined approach as stated.

Compensating controls serve a different purpose than the customized approach. Unlike compensating controls, the customized approach is for entities that choose to meet the requirement in a different manner than what has been written.

Using the customized approach means an entity must meet the stated customized approach objective that is written in the requirements vs. meeting the stated requirement as has always been the case. It's important to note here that if a requirement DOES NOT have a stated customized approach objective within the PCI DSS v4.0 requirements and testing procedures, then the requirement is ineligible for the use of the customized approach – PERIOD.

The customized approach is most successful when the entity to be assessed has mature, repeatable, robust security processes and procedures coupled with strong risk management practices. These kinds of organizations are able to effectively design, document, test, and maintain security controls to meet that objective.

Can I Use a Compensating Control with the Customized Approach?

Well, that's a two-part answer, and the answer could be YES or it could be NO. Now that you're really scratching your head, let's explain:

1. *YES*: A compensating control and the customized approach CAN be used for the same requirement. This could be a situation where certain components, servers, software, etc. (think legacy stuff) would use compensating controls and the customized approach is then used to meet that very same requirement for other system components (think new or bleeding-edge stuff). Let's look at an example:

   a. Requirement 6.3.3 involves patching systems to protect them from known vulnerabilities. Perhaps the entity uses a compensating control to meet

that requirement for a certain type of server where
there is a legitimate and documented business
constraint that prevents that server from meeting
the stated requirement. The entity may also choose
to use the customized approach to meet that
same requirement for other system components,
where it has implemented a unique approach to
ensure components cannot be compromised via
the exploitation of a known vulnerability. Now to
really throw a "monkey wrench" into the mix, the
entity could then use the defined approach to meet
that same requirement for another group of system
components.

b. BREATHE, BREATHE, and you will get what we're
stating in this example. ☺ Basically, the entity has
a breakdown of three different groups of servers.
The first group of servers can meet Requirement
6.3.3 using a compensating control. The second
group of servers will follow the entity's customized
implementation that meets the customized approach
objective for 6.3.3 – which is written as **System
components cannot be compromised via the
exploitation of a known vulnerability**. Finally, the
third group of servers follows the defined approach
as written – NO compensating controls, NO
customized approach – let's call it "PCI Classic."

2. *NO*: Compensating controls are not an option
when using the customized approach to meet
the requirement. The customized approach is
for an entity to develop their own controls that
meet the requirement's customized approach

objective. Again, using our preceding example,
the second group of servers follows a customized
implementation that meets the customized
approach objective for 6.3.3 – which is written as
***System components cannot be compromised via
the exploitation of a known vulnerability***. It would
not make sense for that entity to THEN also develop
an additional, alternative compensating control
because the customized implementation that the
entity developed could not meet the customized
approach objective. In other words, ANY
customized implementation to meet Requirement
6.3.3 MUST meet the customized approach
objective. You can't then "slap" a compensating
control on top of the customized implementation.

Confused yet? I know, it takes some time to wrap your head around it
all. Once you do, it makes perfect sense.

Customized Approach: The Nuts and Bolts

In order to fully understand the use of the customized approach, the
best place to start is PCI DSS v4.0 Requirement 12.3.2, Appendix D, and
Appendix E. These sections of the PCI DSS v4.0 explain fully all that must
be done to use the customized approach including the required targeted
risk analysis, the responsibilities of the entity, and the responsibilities of
the assessor. There are also sample templates with information that must
be included in order to document the customized approach. The following
five entity criteria are taken directly from "PCI DSS Requirements and
Testing Procedures v4.0 Appendix D":

The entity implementing a customized approach must satisfy the following criteria:

- *Document and maintain evidence about each customized control, including all information specified in the Controls Matrix Template in Appendix E1.*

- *Perform and document a targeted risk analysis (PCI DSS Requirement 12.3.2) for each customized control, including all information specified in the Targeted Risk Analysis Template in Appendix E2.*

- *Perform testing of each customized control to prove effectiveness, and document testing performed, methods used, what was tested, when testing was performed, and results of testing in the controls matrix.*

- *Monitor and maintain evidence about the effectiveness of each customized control.*

- *Provide completed controls matrix(es), targeted risk analysis, testing evidence, and evidence of customized control effectiveness to its assessor.*

As you can see, using the customized approach will require quite a bit of effort on the part of the entity. We have discussed previously that only organizations with mature security operations and mature risk operations should attempt to use the customized approach. Perhaps when looking at these five criteria/responsibilities, you can understand why we stated that. Before going into an explanation of the required controls matrix template or the targeted risk analysis and the accompanying targeted risk analysis template, let's look at the four assessor criteria taken directly from "PCI DSS Requirements and Testing Procedures v4.0 Appendix D":

The assessor performing an assessment of customized controls must satisfy the following criteria:

- *Review the entity's controls matrix(es), targeted risk analysis, and evidence of control effectiveness to fully understand the customized control(s) and to verify the entity meets all Customized Approach documentation and evidence requirements.*

- *Derive and document the appropriate testing procedures needed to conduct thorough testing of each customized control.*

- *Test each customized control to determine whether the entity's implementation 1) meets the requirement's Customized Approach Objective and 2) results in an "in place" finding for the requirement.*

- *At all times, QSAs maintain independence requirements defined in the QSA Qualification Requirements. This means if a QSA is involved in designing or implementing a customized control, that QSA does not also derive testing procedures for, assess, or assist with the assessment of that customized control.*

Again, the use of a customized approach will require more effort from assessors than was previously required when an entity could only validate using the defined approach with or without any compensating controls.

There is more information contained in "PCI DSS Requirements and Testing Procedures v4.0 Appendix D" that helps explain the symbiotic relationship an entity and an assessor will need to use in order to pull off using the customized approach and do it correctly. Here is the rest of "PCI DSS Requirements and Testing Procedures v4.0 Appendix D":

The entity and its assessor are expected to work together to ensure 1) they agree that the customized control(s) fully meets the customized approach objective, 2) the assessor fully understands the customized control, and 3) the entity understands the derived testing the assessor will perform.

Use of the customized approach must be completed by a QSA or ISA and documented in accordance with instructions in the Report on Compliance (ROC) Template and following the instructions in the FAQs for use with PCI DSS v4.0 ROC Template available on the PCI SSC website.

Entities that complete a Self-Assessment Questionnaire are not eligible to use a customized approach; however, these entities may elect to have a QSA or ISA perform their assessment and document it in a ROC Template.

The use of the customized approach may be regulated by organizations that manage compliance programs (for example, payment brands and acquirers). Therefore, questions about use of a customized approach must be referred to those organizations, including, for example, whether an entity is required to use a QSA, or may use an ISA to complete an assessment using the customized approach.

Note: *Compensating controls are not an option with the customized approach. Because the customized approach allows an entity to determine and design the controls needed to meet a requirement's Customized Approach Objective, the entity is expected to effectively implement the controls it designed for that requirement without needing to also implement alternate, compensating controls.*

After reading this information, one can glean two very important points to make here:

1. Entities documenting PCI validation using one of the Self-Assessment Questionnaires (SAQ) are ineligible to use the customized approach – only the Report on Compliance (ROC) can be used for the customized approach.

2. The card brands and acquirers may have certain rules as to the use of the customized approach. This means ANY entity that wants to use the customized approach to meet any requirement(s) should contact the card brands (if a service provider) or the acquirer of record (if a merchant) before using this approach. It would be a shame for an organization to decide to use the customized approach and spend time documenting it, validating it, and then submitting the ROC to either the brands or an acquirer and be told "We don't accept a customized approach for that requirement" or something to that effect.

Customized Approach: The Templates

As was stated earlier, there are two areas where use of new templates is required when using the customized approach to validate a requirement. First, it will be necessary for the entity to fully document the approach using a controls matrix. Second, ANY use of the customized approach will dictate the entity perform a targeted risk analysis and document it using a targeted risk analysis template. The following information comes directly from "PCI DSS Requirements and Testing Procedures v4.0 Appendix E":

Appendix E Sample Templates to Support Customized Approach

This appendix contains example templates for the controls matrix and a targeted risk analysis, to be documented by the entity as part of the customized approach. These templates are examples of formats that could be used.

E1 Sample Controls Matrix Template

The following is a sample controls matrix template that an entity may use to document their customized implementation.

As described in Appendix D: Customized Approach, entities using the customized approach must complete a controls matrix to provide details for each implemented control that explain what is implemented, how the entity has determined that the controls meet the stated objective of a PCI DSS requirement, how the control provides at least the equivalent level of protection as would be achieved by meeting the defined requirement, and how the entity has assurance about the effectiveness of the control on an ongoing basis.

The assessor uses the information within each controls matrix to plan and prepare for the assessment.

This sample controls matrix template includes the minimum information to be documented by the entity and provided to the assessor for a customized validation. While it is not required that this specific template be used, it is required that the entity's customized approach documentation includes all information defined in this template, and that the entity provides this exact information to its assessor.

The controls matrix does not replace the need for the assessor to independently develop appropriate testing procedures for validating the implemented controls. *The assessor must still perform the necessary testing to verify the controls meet the objective of the requirement, are effective, and are properly maintained. The controls matrix also does not replace the reporting requirements for customized validations as specified in the ROC Template.*

The controls matrix must include at least the information in the following table.

Sample Controls Matrix Template for PCI DSS Requirements met via the Customized Approach To be completed by the entity being assessed		
Customized control name/identifier	<Entity defines how they want to refer to this control>	
PCI DSS Requirement(s) number and objective(s) that is met with this control(s)	Requirement #: Requirement #:	Objective: Objective:

Sample Controls Matrix Template for PCI DSS Requirements met via the Customized Approach To be completed by the entity being assessed	
Details of control(s)	
What is the implemented control(s)?	\<Entity describes what the control is and what it does\>
Where is the control(s) implemented?	\<Entity identifies locations of facilities and system components where control is implemented and managed\>
When is the control(s) performed?	\<Entity details how frequently the control is performed – for example, runs continuously in real time or is scheduled to run at NN times and at XX intervals\>
Who has overall responsibility and accountability for the control(s)?	\<Entity includes details of individual personnel/roles with responsibility and accountability for this control\>
Who is involved in managing, maintaining, and monitoring the control(s)?	\<Entity includes details of individual personnel/roles and/or teams, as applicable, that manage, maintain, and monitor the control\>
For each PCI DSS requirement the control(s) is used for, the entity provides details of the following:	
Entity describes how the implemented control(s) meets the stated *Customized Approach Objective* of the PCI DSS requirement.	\<Entity describes how the control meets the stated customized approach objective of the PCI DSS requirement, and summarizes related results\>
Entity describes testing **it performed** and the results of that testing that demonstrates the control(s) meets the objective of the applicable requirement.	\<Entity describes the testing it performed to prove the control meets the stated objective of the PCI DSS requirement, and summarizes related results\>
Entity briefly describes the results of the separate targeted risk analysis **it performed** that explains the control(s) implemented and describes how the results verify the control(s) provides at least an equivalent level of protection as the defined approach for the applicable PCI DSS requirement. *See the separate Targeted Risk Analysis Template for details on how to document this risk analysis.*	\<Entity briefly describes the results of its risk analysis for this control, which is detailed separately in the Targeted Risk Analysis\>

Sample Controls Matrix Template for PCI DSS Requirements met via the Customized Approach To be completed by the entity being assessed	
Entity describes the measures **it has implemented** to ensure the control(s) is maintained and its effectiveness is assured on an ongoing basis. *For example, how the entity monitors for control effectiveness, how control failures are detected and responded to, and the actions taken.*	\<Entity describes how it ensures the control is maintained and how the control's effectiveness is assured.\>

As you can see, this will require a lot of work on the part of the entity to document the controls matrix properly before providing the information to the assessor. The assessor will then need to independently develop appropriate testing procedures for validating the implemented controls. The requirements also include a template to be used by the assessor.

The following template is also in Appendix E, but NOT in the "PCI DSS Requirements and Testing Procedures v4.0" that we have been using so far. Rather, the assessor template is located in "PCI DSS v4.0 ROC Template r1 Appendix E." Here is that template:

CHAPTER 16   THE CUSTOMIZED APPROACH, COMPENSATING CONTROLS, AND THE TARGETED RISK ANALYSIS

Identify the **customized control name / identifier** for each control used to meet the Customized Approach Objective. *(Note: use the Customized Control name from the assessed entity's controls matrix)*	<Enter Response Here>
Describe each control used to meet the Customized Approach Objective. *(Note: Refer to the Payment Card Industry Data Security Standard (PCI DSS) Requirements and Testing Procedures for the Customized Approach Objective)*	<Enter Response Here>
Describe how the control(s) meet the Customized Approach Objective.	<Enter Response Here>
Identify the **Controls Matrix documentation** reviewed that supports a customized approach for this requirement.	<Enter Response Here>
Identify the **Targeted Risk Analysis documentation** reviewed that supports the customized approach for this requirement.	<Enter Response Here>
Identify name(s) of the assessor(s) who attests that: • The entity completed the Controls Matrix including all information specified in the Controls Matrix Template in Appendix E1 of *Payment Card Industry Data Security Standard (PCI DSS) Requirements and Testing Procedures* and the results of the Controls Matrix support the customized approach for this requirement. • The entity completed the Targeted Risk Analysis including all information specified in the Targeted Risk Analysis Template in Appendix E2 of *Payment Card Industry Data Security Standard (PCI DSS) Requirements and Testing Procedures*, and that the results of the Risk Analysis support use of the customized approach for this requirement.	<Report Name(s) of Assessor(s) Here>

Describe the testing procedures derived and performed by the assessor to validate that the **implemented controls meet the Customized Approach Objective**; for example, whether the customized control(s) is sufficiently robust to provide at least an equivalent level of protection as provided by the defined approach.

Note 1: Technical reviews (for example, reviewing configuration settings, operating effectiveness, etc.) should be performed where possible and appropriate.

Note 2: Add additional rows for each assessor-derived testing procedure, as needed. Ensure that all rows to the right of the "Assessor-derived testing procedure" are copied for each assessor-derived testing procedure that is added.

<Assessor-derived testing procedure>	**Identify** what was tested (for example, individuals interviewed, system components reviewed, processes observed, etc.) *Note: all items tested must be uniquely identified.*	<Enter Response Here>
	Identify all evidence examined for this testing procedure.	<Enter Response Here>
	Describe the results of the testing performed by the assessor for this testing procedure and how these results verify the implemented controls meet the Customized Approach Objective.	<Enter Response Here>

Document the testing procedures derived and performed by the assessor to validate the **controls are maintained to ensure ongoing effectiveness**; for example, how the entity monitors for control effectiveness and how control failures are detected, responded to, and the actions taken.

Note 1: Technical reviews (for example, reviewing configuration settings, operating effectiveness, etc.) should be performed where possible and appropriate.

Note 2: Add additional rows for each assessor-derived testing procedure, as needed. Ensure that all rows to the right of the "Assessor-derived testing procedure" are copied for each assessor-derived testing procedure that is added.

<Assessor-derived testing procedure>	**Identify** what was tested (for example, individuals interviewed, system components reviewed, processes observed, etc.) *Note: all items tested must be uniquely identified.*	<Enter Response Here>
	Identify all evidence examined for this testing procedure.	<Enter Response Here>
	Describe the results of the testing performed by the assessor for this testing procedure and how these results verify the implemented controls are maintained to ensure ongoing effectiveness.	<Enter Response Here>

It's important to note that this template must be used by the assessor
to document each instance where a customized control is used to meet a
PCI DSS requirement. However, assessors must also document validation
at the corresponding PCI DSS requirement in "Part II. Findings and
Observations" of the ROC template.

Customized Approach: Independent Responsibilities

After looking at these templates and realizing there needs to be CLEAR
separation between the entity and the assessor when each is developing
the data for these templates, one can see that use of the customized
approach, while perhaps VERY useful for some entities, will present a lot of
work for other entities and assessors.

"Why?" you ask. Because typically assessors and entities work together
a lot when validating an entity's PCI compliance, and it's generally not
an issue, as the defined approach was the method of the day. Now, using
this new customized approach means the entity has to come up with
the controls and the implementation, management, maintenance, and
monitoring for said controls. The assessor can have NO involvement
with any of those efforts and still be able to show any real integrity when
validating everything.

The assessor will be charged with developing test procedures and
must maintain independence. If an assessor is involved in designing or
implementing a customized control, that assessor cannot derive testing
procedures for, assess, or assist with the assessment of that customized
control. PERIOD.

Targeted Risk Analysis

One of the items we mentioned earlier "in passing" was the use of a "targeted risk analysis." It's true that all entities using the customized approach to validation will be required to perform and document a targeted risk analysis (PCI DSS Requirement 12.3.2) for each requirement customized control they develop. Just stating this is true seems trite when you realize what this means.

It may be important to note that the three words **targeted risk analysis** appear in the "Payment Card Industry Data Security Standard Requirements and Testing Procedures v4.0" on 20 individual pages, containing 52 occurrences of that phrase. This phrase has 44 occurrences within the "PCI DSS v4.0 ROC Template r1." Perhaps we need to explore the what and how of the "targeted risk analysis."

WHAT: Appendix G in "Payment Card Industry Data Security Standard Requirements and Testing Procedures v4.0" contains a PCI glossary, and the official definition for a targeted risk analysis states

> *For PCI DSS purposes, a risk analysis that focuses on a specific PCI DSS requirement(s) of interest, either because the requirement allows flexibility (for example, as to frequency) or, for the Customized Approach, to explain how the entity assessed the risk and determined the customized control meets the objective of a PCI DSS requirement.*

So now we know that a targeted risk analysis will be needed when a requirement has a "frequency" of accomplishment, and previously the PCI requirements would use a word like **periodically** to define the frequency of something being done. This will not be the case now. Let's look at an example. In PCI DSS v3.2.1, Requirement 9.9.2 relates to merchants with payment devices to inspect them. The requirement states

> *9.9.2 Periodically inspect device surfaces to detect tampering (for example, addition of card skimmers to devices), or substitution (for example, by checking the serial number or other device characteristics to verify it has not been swapped with a fraudulent device).*

Notice the use of that word "periodically." Well, I don't know about you, but that could mean hourly, weekly, daily, monthly, yearly, etc. Let's now look at the same requirement as it has been written in PCI DSS v4.0. The new requirement that applies is 9.5.1.2.1 and states

> *9.5.1.2.1 The frequency of periodic POI device inspections and the type of inspections performed is defined in the entity's targeted risk analysis, which is performed according to all elements specified in Requirement 12.3.1.*

Can this defined inspection period still mean hourly, weekly, daily, monthly, yearly, etc.? Well, YES, actually. However, it will now be the entity's responsibility to conduct a targeted risk analysis to "defend" the defined period in accordance with the risk associated with said frequency of inspection.

We also know that use of the customized approach will require the use of a targeted risk analysis. Let's now look at the actual requirements in PCI DSS v4.0 that formerly discuss risk:

> *12.3.1 Each PCI DSS requirement that provides flexibility for how frequently it is performed (for example, requirements to be performed periodically) is supported by a targeted risk analysis.*

> *12.3.2 A targeted risk analysis is performed for each PCI DSS requirement that the entity meets with the customized approach.*

12.3.3 Cryptographic cipher suites and protocols in use are documented and reviewed at least once every 12 months.

12.3.4 Hardware and software technologies in use are reviewed at least once every 12 months.

Note   Requirements 12.3.1, 12.3.3, and 12.3.4 are considered best practices until March 31, 2025, after which time they will be required and must be fully considered during a PCI DSS assessment. There has been a joke among the assessor community that many QSA and ISA personnel may "leave" or "quit" the PCI assessment world on March 30, 2025. ☺

The important point to be made here is that there is no future date for targeted risk analysis when it relates to use of the customized approach. As soon as an entity decides to use the customized approach for any requirement, it WILL entail a targeted risk analysis be performed in order to ensure the entity's implementation will fully meet the stated customized approach objective that is written in the requirement.

So that's sort of the WHAT of a targeted risk analysis, and as one can see, there will be some work needed on the part of the entity being assessed to get through it. So let's attempt to look at the HOW of a targeted risk analysis.

HOW: Performing a risk analysis is not something new. Basically there are more than a zillion different risk models, risk templates, risk descriptions, risk implementation guides, etc. With any risk model, guide, etc., generally these are the four basic steps one must follow:

1.   Identify risk.

2.   Assess risk.

3.   Treat risk.

4.   Monitor risk.

The PCI DSS v4.0 provides a template that can be used for the targeted risk analysis. It is located in "Payment Card Industry Data Security Standard Requirements and Testing Procedures v4.0 Appendix E2." It is actually very comprehensive and at the same time not too difficult to understand and complete. It's also a very important document for the assessor to use when validating the entity. Here's the actual wording and the template:

E2 Sample Targeted Risk Analysis Template

The following is a sample targeted risk analysis template an entity may use for their customized implementation.

As described in Appendix D: Customized Approach and in accordance with PCI DSS Requirement 12.3.2, an entity using the customized approach must provide a detailed targeted risk analysis for each requirement the entity is meeting with the customized approach. The risk analysis defines the risk, evaluates the effect on security if the defined requirement is not met, and describes how the entity has determined that the controls provide at least an equivalent level of protection as provided by the defined PCI DSS requirement.

The assessor uses the information in the targeted risk analysis to plan and prepare for the assessment.

In completing a targeted risk analysis for a customized approach, it is important to remember that:

- *The asset being protected is the cardholder data that is stored, processed, or transmitted by the entity.*

- *The threat actor is highly motivated and capable. The motivation and capability of threat actors tends to increase in relation to the volume of cardholder data that a successful attack will realize.*

- *The likelihood that an entity will be targeted by threat actors increases as the entity stores, processes, or transmits greater volumes of cardholder data.*

- *The mischief is directly related to the objective. For example, if the objective is "malicious software cannot execute", the mischief is that malicious software executes; if the objective is "day-to-day responsibilities for performing all the activities are allocated", the mischief is that the responsibilities are not allocated.*

Note   *The term "mischief" as used in this targeted risk analysis (for example, in 1.3 in the table below) refers to an occurrence or event that negatively affects the security posture of the entity. Examples of this are the absence of a policy, the failure to conduct a vulnerability scan, or that malware executes in the entity's environment.*

This sample targeted risk analysis template includes the minimum information to be documented by the entity and provided to the assessor for a customized validation. While it is not required that this specific template be used, it is required that the entity's customized approach documentation include all information defined in this template, and that the entity provides this exact information to its assessor.

The targeted risk analysis must include at least the information in the following table.

Sample Targeted Risk Analysis for PCI DSS Requirements met via the Customized Approach	
To be completed by the entity being assessed	
Item	**Details**
1. Identify the requirement	
1.1 Identify the PCI DSS requirement as written.	<Entity identifies the requirement>
1.2 Identify the objective of the PCI DSS requirement as written.	<Entity identifies the objective of the requirement>
1.3 Describe the mischief that the requirement was designed to prevent	<Entity describes the mischief>
	<Entity describes the effect on its security if the objective is not successfully met by the entity.>
	<Entity describes which security fundamentals would not be in place, or what a threat actor may be able to do if the objective is not successfully met by the entity.>
2. Describe the proposed solution	
2.1 Customized control name/identifier	<Entity identifies the customized control as documented in the Controls Matrix.>
2.2 What parts of the requirement as written will change in the proposed solution?	<Entity identifies what elements of the requirement will not be met by the defined approach and so will be covered by customized approach. This could be as small as changing the periodicity of a requirement, or the implementation of a completely different set of controls to meet the objective.>
2.3 How will the proposed solution prevent the mischief?	<Entity describes how the controls detailed in the Controls Matrix will prevent the mischief identified in 1.3.>

Sample Targeted Risk Analysis for PCI DSS Requirements met via the Customized Approach					
To be completed by the entity being assessed					
Item	**Details**				
3. Analyze any changes to the LIKELIHOOD of the mischief occurring, leading to a breach in confidentiality of cardholder data					
3.1 Describe the factors detailed in the Control Matrix that affect the likelihood of the mischief occurring.	Entity describes: • How successful the controls will be at preventing the mischief • How the controls detailed in the Control Matrix reduce the likelihood of the mischief occurring				
3.2 Describe the reasons the mischief may still occur after the application of the customized control.	Entity describes: • The typical reasons for the control to fail, the likelihood of this, and how could it be prevented • How resilient the entity's processes and systems are for detecting that the control(s) are not operating normally? • How a threat actor could bypass this control – what steps would they need to take, how hard is it, would the threat actor be detected before the control failed? How has this been determined?				
3.3 To what extent do the controls detailed in the customized approach represent a change in the likelihood of the mischief occurring when compared with the defined approach requirement?	Mischief more likely to occur	☐	No change	☐	Mischief less likely to occur	☐
3.4 Provide the reasoning for your assessment of the change in likelihood that the mischief occurs once the customized controls are in place.	Entity provides: • The justification for the assessment documented at 3.3. • The criteria and values used for the assessment documented at 3.3.				

240

Sample Targeted Risk Analysis for PCI DSS Requirements met via the Customized Approach To be completed by the entity being assessed				
Item	**Details**			
4. Analyze any changes to the IMPACT of unauthorized access to account data				
4.1 For the scope of system components that this solution covers what volume of account data would be at risk of unauthorized access if the solution failed?	**4.1.1** Number of stored PANs	*Maximum at any one time*	**4.1.2** Number of PANs processed or transmitted over a 12-month period	*Total*
4.2 Description of how the customized controls will directly: • Reduce the number of individual PANs compromised if a threat actor is successful, and/or • Allow quicker notification of the PANs compromised to the card brands.	Impact to the payment ecosystem is directly related to the number of accounts compromised and how quickly any compromised PANs can be blocked by the card issuer. Entity describes how the customized controls achieve the following if any of the customized controls: • Reduce the volume of cardholder data that is stored, processed, or transmitted and therefore reduce what is available to a successful threat actor, and/or • Decrease the time to detection, notification of compromised accounts, and containment of the threat actor.			
5. Risk approval and review				
5.1 I have reviewed the above risk analysis and I agree that the use of the proposed customized approach as detailed provides at least an equivalent level of protection as the defined approach for the applicable PCI DSS requirement.	A member of executive management must review and agree to the proposed customized approach. <Member of entity's executive management signs that it reviewed and agreed to the customized approach documented herein.>			
5.2 This risk analysis must be reviewed and updated no later than:	The risk analysis should be reviewed at least every twelve months and more frequently if the customized approach itself is time limited (for example, because there is a planned change in technology) or if other factors dictate a needed change. In the event of an unscheduled risk review, detail the reason the review occurred. <Entity indicates date the targeted risk analysis was reviewed and updated.>			

Any entity needing to perform a targeted risk analysis can simply follow this template, document it completely, and then provide it to the assessor. The assessor will then need to fully review this analysis document and decide if it indeed is accurate as to the risk associated with use of the customized approach for the particular requirement in question. The assessor has to take into consideration the customized approach objective as written for the requirement, the approach and controls the entity has presented, and the risk associated with everything.

Index

A

Access, 50, 56, 105–107, 119, 148, 159, 165, 213

Access control
concepts
least privilege, 97
need to know, 96, 97

Access control model, 100, 101, 103, 105, 111

Access control systems, 99, 100, 104, 108, 109

Access payment card data, 101, 103

Account data storage, 47, 48

Action Plan, non-compliant Requirements, 209

Active Directory, 105, 108, 119, 120, 125

Anti-malware mechanisms, 78, 80

Anti-malware policy, 76

Anti-malware software, 74–77, 79, 80

Anti-malware solutions, 75, 77–80

Anti-phishing, 75, 80

Anti-spoofing measures, 23

Applicable vulnerabilities, 170, 173

Application ID, 112, 114

Applications, 8, 42, 74, 81, 90, 136, 185, 215, 222

Application security assessment tools, 83, 171

Approved Scanning Vendor (ASV), 2, 3, 175

Assessor, 8, 128, 221, 227, 228, 234, 238, 241

Assessor Quality Management (AQM) process, 4

Attestation of Compliance (AOC), 3
documented evidence, 207
non-compliance conditions, 209
Part 2a, 207, 208
Part 2d, 208
Part 3, 209
Part 4, 209
PCI assessment, 207
QSA, 209
service providers, 207, 208, 210

Audit logs
anomalies/suspicious activity detection, 160
anomalies/suspicious activity identification, 162
destruction and unauthorized modifications protection, 161

© Arthur B. Cooper Jr., Jeff Hall, David Mundhenk, Ben Rothke 2023
A. B. Cooper Jr. et al., *The Definitive Guide to PCI DSS Version 4*,
https://doi.org/10.1007/978-1-4842-9288-4

T

Printed in the United States
by Baker & Taylor Publisher Services

Printed in the United States
by Baker & Taylor Publisher Services